What shall we do with Mother?

What shall we do with Mother?

What to do when your elderly parent is dependent on you

Rosie Staal

Editors Richard Craze, Roni Jay

new tricks for old dogs

Published by White Ladder Press Ltd
Great Ambrook, Near Ipplepen, Devon TQ12 5UL
01803 813343
www.whiteladderpress.com

First published in Great Britain in 2006

10 9 8 7 6 5 4 3 2 1

© Rosie Staal 2006

The right of Rosie Staal to be identified as author of this work has been asserted by her in accordance with the Copyright, Designs and Patents Act 1988.

ISBN 1 905410 03 4
ISBN 978 1 905410 03 3

British Library Cataloguing in Publication Data
A CIP record for this book can be obtained from the British Library.

Designed and typeset by Julie Martin Ltd
Cover design by Julie Martin Ltd
Cover photograph by Jonathon Bosley
Cover model Alice Llewellyn
Printed and bound by TJ International Ltd, Padstow, Cornwall

White Ladder Press
Great Ambrook, Near Ipplepen, Devon TQ12 5UL
01803 813343
www.whiteladderpress.com

Contents

Acknowledgements

A number of people have generously shared their experiences and their knowledge with me, not least a small army of carers whose contributions have been invaluable. I acknowledge their desire for anonymity and I thank them with the utmost sincerity – and humility.

Thanks are due to the professionals I consulted, including Elizabeth Bartlett, of the Salisbury branch of the Alzheimer's Society, Carol Bunnagar, Vice-chairman of Age Concern Blandford Forum, and Helen Joyce, of the Winchester and Andover Carer Centre of The Princess Royal Trust for Carers.

I am indebted to my sister, Caroline, for a constant flow of useful information, and to good friends Carla Benedict and Emma Ryder Richardson for pointing me in the right direction on occasions. My warmest gratitude also goes to Pam Ferris and Claire Rayner for their enthusiasm for this book and their kind words of encouragement.

My mother deserves heartfelt thanks for going beyond the call of maternal duty and generously sharing the results of her highly original lateral thinking.

Above all, I am deeply grateful to David, my husband, for his wisdom, immense patience and support throughout the writing of this book.

Foreword

"There is nothing so powerful as an idea whose time has come" – I can't remember who said that, but it certainly applies to this book. Because of our aging population more and more people are wondering 'What shall we do with Mother?' and I've been one of them – twice!

When I looked after my mother in the early 1980s it was a pretty lonely business. The rest of the family were miles away – mainly in Australia – and I was a single actress living in a grotty flat in the East End of London, not an ideal place in which to look after an invalid. Luckily, my mother and I had a fantastic relationship right to the end. We were united in viewing her illness as a common enemy. Unfortunately, it sometimes felt like the National Health Service was a common enemy too.

More recently my husband and I have had to deal with the slow deterioration of his mother from Alzheimer's. The years leading up to the realisation that she had the disease, and her final placement in a suitable home, were particularly stressful, and my sympathy goes out to anyone who has been in this situation. My husband describes it as 'living on orange alert'.

So I gladly accept the title of 'Two Time Ofcap' (offspring caring for an aged parent), as coined by Rosie.

In both these life passages I would have benefited greatly from reading this book. The case histories cover a wide range of experience and I'm sure most people will find something that resonates with their own life.

Every family situation is different and there is no such thing as a typical carer. In fact, a great deal of the work of The Princess Royal Trust for Carers – the organisation I know best – is to help people to recognise and accept this label. This is the first step towards breaking the isolation and showing them the various forms of help that are available. I think of this book in the same way.

So I doff my cap to Ofcaps everywhere. May your support be steadfast and your journey smooth.

Pam Ferris
Vice-president, The Princess Royal Trust for Carers

INTRODUCTION

Into the unknown

It could be the constant clutching of a tear soaked hanky or perhaps it's the confusion over which way up to hold the TV remote that paints the more poignant picture of the newly widowed. One illustrates the emotional turmoil, the other the bewilderment of coping with everyday practicalities.

Being cast adrift in a great ocean of the unknown is particularly alarming when life up to this point has been a partnership. Having to face a future alone, without the other complementary half, can make daily living so daunting as to seem impossible.

This is where you come in. All you have to do is cast off the mantle of the overgrown child and acquire the air and authority of the One Who Knows Best, the worldly, capable and caring son or daughter whose wise words and thoughtful actions will ease the burdens of the afflicted and comfort their tormented souls. Not much to ask, is it? You've plenty of time to transform yourself – let's say 24 hours, though try and make the change more quickly, say overnight, if possible.

The transformation complete, and your head full of useful information about benefits, tax allowances, bereavement counsellors, old people's clubs, the nutritional value of ready meals for one and singles' coach holidays to the bulbfields of Holland, you impart the knowledge like the Angel Gabriel and wait for the round of applause and speech of thanks.

It doesn't come. All this, you see, is expected of you. It's not that you are being taken for granted, it's just that, whereas yesterday you were Our Child, today you're My Son or My Daughter, the one to be depended on. The tables have been turned, the role reversal is complete.

Alongside this new role run all your other duties, so that what you now have to look forward to is a life as the filling in a rather uncomfortable sandwich, with pressure from both sides, a parent at the top, the rest of the family underneath. Being pushed and pulled, if not torn, in all directions is one thing when you're young and energetic, but this role as the hapless piggy in the middle, the pivotal focus of two, or perhaps three, generations of the family, more often comes to us in later life, at the very time when a little slowing of the pace is not only expected but eagerly anticipated.

The little cameos are unmistakable, whether we spot them in the supermarket, at the school sports day, walking in the woods or even on holiday: they are the man or woman of middle years supporting an older version of themselves, patting a hand reassuringly, enunciating clearly, cajoling gently, smiling encouragingly, all the while playing out a role that is familiar because, in so many cases, they relied on support like this when they were toddlers.

Stepping up a gear in middle age to accommodate the needs of an ageing parent involves both physical and mental adjustment. Life will never be the same again when you take on the responsibility of someone else's welfare, but neither is it likely to be dull and uneventful, as the stories in this book will show.

We will follow the lives of a number of men and women who are newly dependent, through widowhood, illness or increasing age and frailty, their stories told in part through their daughters or sons upon whom the mantle of Number One Carer has fallen, whether they like it or not. They are the new generation of Offspring Caring for an Aged Parent, what we'll call Ofcaps. Many of these devoted Ofcaps play their part, and more, through love for their dependent parent. Others admit they have simply done what they see as their duty, knowing it is expected of them, but without a great deal of affection on either side.

In between are those who are muddling through, driven by instinct, compassion, and an awareness that, in the blink of an eye, it's going to be their turn. What they're doing is what they hope their children may never have to do for them, but if they do, then their turn of duty has been a blueprint, perhaps a down payment for a comfortable old age.

Every story gives an insight into a life which in the main is lived unnoticed, for these carers are among the quietly capable heroes and heroines, thousands and thousands of them, who step in to take on the responsibility for the life of the one who, years ago, gave them life. The overriding feeling that most Ofcaps have in common is not pride or satisfaction in the way they are coping, but guilt. Guilt that they're not more competent, guilt that they can't do more, guilt that they sometimes feel resentful, guilt that they get short tempered, guilt that they can't make their parent better or happier, guilt that they don't live closer, guilt that they should or shouldn't have asked their parent to move in with them, guilt that they're feeling well when their parent isn't, and guilt that they feel guilty when a hundred people have told them they shouldn't.

Few would ever say that being a closely involved Ofcap is all hard work and no payback. Many speak of the wonderful closeness they enjoy with a parent they last knew properly when they still lived at home, and in those days, possibly as much as 40 or 50 years ago, it may have been a prickly relationship with occasional stand-offs over staying out too late and unsuitable hairstyles. Now, with the benefit of maturity, the Ofcap can learn about their parent as an individual and forge a rewarding relationship based on a perfect kind of love.

Changes in the relationship between parent and child as both grow older are complex and subtle, and in virtually all cases there is that shift of power that comes with the responsibility for the welfare of Mum or Dad.

The turnaround is recorded in a particularly poignant way by Philip Roth in his book *Patrimony*, which evokes the last years of his father's life. The son writes: "I then spoke four words to (my father), four words that I'd never uttered to him before in my life. 'Do as *I* say,' I told him. 'Put on a sweater and your walking shoes.'

"And they worked, those four words. I am 55, he is almost 87, and the year is 1988. 'Do as *I* say,' I tell him and he does it. The end of one era, the dawn of another."

Ofcaps have to make that shift, from *ask* to *order,* from '*please*' to '*do it*' when talking with an elderly parent. They have to cajole, confer, direct, act competent and confident, wondering all the time if these are the right decisions and if they're doing the right thing.

Of course it is not your role to make decisions for your parent. As far as it is possible and reasonable, decisions should be made *with* a parent. It is sometimes easy to forget that, to overlook the need to ask, being too impatient to wait for an answer delivered with halting speech.

When decisions are difficult or problems insuperable, the inclination is for Ofcaps to feel frustrated, helpless, guilty and responsible. But you can't solve everything. You are not superhuman. Do the best you can and, if that isn't enough, seek help.

An important factor in establishing a harmonious relationship has to do with Mum or Dad accepting the Ofcap's involvement. Some parents are quite relaxed about the transfer of responsibility and are relieved to be taken care of. Others – and these are usually the more independent parents who have been easier to deal with all along – can become more difficult when the need for help is obvious. Ofcaps, however well-meaning and kind-hearted, can be perceived as meddling and irksome. There is a balance to be struck and it isn't easy.

This present generation of Ofcaps is something of a phenomenon. With so many more people surviving into old age, and with fewer large families, the proportion of young to old has undergone a significant shift in the past 50 years. The population of over 80s for example, the fastest growing age group in the UK, is expected to double to 5 million by 2031, according to the Office of National Statistics. In line with this, the demand for places in residential and nursing homes is likely to increase threefold.

Hitherto, people either didn't live long enough to create this predicament, or they were consigned like sad parcels to unravel over time in institutional care. Now, with improved geriatric medicine and about two-thirds of long stay geriatric NHS beds closed down (nearly 51,000 were taken away between 1987 and 2001 alone), families and care homes are having to fill the gap. And it's the Ofcaps who are, understandably, the first port of call and who are therefore taking the greater burden and for a longer period.

The classic vision of an Ofcap is of a woman, possibly single but certainly without the impediments of children or a job, contentedly caring for her sweet old mother, the two of them sharing three regular meals of home-cooked food daily and sitting contentedly completing jigsaws and embroidering fire-screens before going upstairs for an undisturbed night's sleep. Switch to reality, and you'll find that Ofcaps come in all ages, all stages of life and in male and female versions. Their mothers, or fathers, may be old but they aren't usually sweet, mealtimes are chaotic, messy and irregular, food is rarely home cooked because there isn't time to peel a potato let alone boil one, and the thought of keeping twitchy hands occupied with jigsaws and sewing needles is laughable when you think of the consequences. Instead, there's high decibel television to be watched and carped about, and then it's time for the tedious, tetchy, interminable routine that precedes the blessed moment of lights out. And even then, the Ofcap remains on edge, ever ready throughout the night to spring into action, reacting to that imperious call, that demanding ring of the bell, that timid cry, when no-one else will do but you.

Most Ofcaps aren't even under the same roof as Mother or Father, but they can still experience some of those same feelings of pressure, anxiety, bewilderment and helplessness. It's a tough call being an Ofcap. Tougher still when you're an Ofcap, as so many are, with additional demands of job and family. One Ofcap describes that situation as like being 'in the middle of a tug o' war rope being pulled this way and that until you're left reeling, face down in the dirt'. Others call them the more important sounding Pivotal Generation.

Statistics to keep you awake at night while you ponder whether a long and happy retirement could ever be yours, include the following:

- About two million of the six million carers in the UK are aged 65 or over, and about 400,000 of them care for a parent

- More than one-third of people in the UK will become carers – of a family member or friend – at some stage in their lives

- There are two million new carers every year and by 2037 that number is expected to have risen to nine million every year

- For someone aged 24 now, the chances of being a carer will treble by the time they are aged 59

- By 2037, it is almost inevitable that someone aged 30-54 will be a carer for an older person

So the chances are that if you're not an Ofcap now, you are more than likely to be at some time.

This book is intended to help you as a friend who has been there before. It is a book of experiences, not a book of reference. Its purpose is to reassure Ofcaps that they are not alone, and to give them comfort and strength as they take on new responsibilities that had once seemed so far in the future but which are suddenly here, now.

* The characters in this book are real but their names have been changed to protect their privacy

CHAPTER 1

Home alone

The party's over. The glasses and cups have been washed and put away, the cake crumbs swept up and the chairs put back in their correct places. Everyone has said their goodbyes and left.

'Well then, Mother,' says the exhausted hostess as she removes her apron. 'What on earth are we going to do with you?'

Mother is on her own now. The crowd of friends and fairly distant relatives who have just left the house have done their duty, they've paid their respects to the dear departed one, availed themselves of the widow's hospitality, given her a hug and a promise to keep in touch, and returned to their homes.

The house feels empty now they've gone. It's going to feel emptier tomorrow, when Mother's immediate family, her son and her daughter, both in their late 40s, will have driven away and left her, up to her neck in grief and loneliness. And how will they feel, in their grief, too, as they wave goodbye?

The terrible helplessness of loss, the aching chasms of emptiness created by the death of a loved one, affect people in different ways, but for the one left behind, left in the four walls that suddenly seem more hostile than familiar, the sensations can be overwhelming. There is absolutely no mistaking the fact that there's a space in the bed where so recently there was a living, breathing person. Someone so dear and so loved and so much a fixed point as to seem almost, yet never, there.

'So what are we going to do with you, Mother?' asks the son, unaware the same question has just been asked by his sister.

Let's not talk about it now, the three of them agree, so the subject gets dropped. It is picked up again every time the son and daughter speak to each other over the coming months. It's one way of sharing the burden, but they are stumped for an answer. They agree in the end that the answer will probably come from Mother herself.

In the meantime, Mother must come to terms with being that delicate creature officially referred to, on countless forms and documents that demand her attention, as A Widow. It's all official now. There's no turning back on this uncomfortable ride into the unknown, alone.

The very fact Mother is on her own usually rallies the family and new routines can be established where visiting, staying, going on outings and sometimes even joining in with holidays can become a comforting sort of substitute for the previous way of life as a couple. Feeling cared for and loved is important in the healing process during bereavement, and family, especially, play a crucial role because Father can be spoken of freely as memories are shared.

Some widows and widowers cry so much they keep Kleenex in business. Others maintain dignity and a stiff upper lip on all occasions, their emotions securely buttoned up. Corked or uncorked, grief displays itself in a multitude of ways and can be an early test of ability for new Ofcaps as they, too, start to learn how to cope under pressure.

It is helpful to be aware of the various stages of bereavement and grieving and to bear in mind that intense emotions and swift changes in mood are normal. Don't panic and think your Mum or Dad is losing their marbles.

Emotional numbness is often the first reaction to a loss, lasting anything from a few hours to a few weeks. Strangely, it can be a welcome reaction because it can help you and your family achieve all that has to be done in the way of practical arrangements. Remember, if people tell you how well your Mum or Dad is bearing up, it's probably the numbness that's carrying them through. Don't kid yourself that they'll be the exception who takes it all in their stride and enrols on a scuba-diving course next week.

Look out for the next stage: a deep yearning for the lost partner. They may show this by being angry or agitated, finding it hard to concentrate, relax or sleep. They could also tell you how guilty they feel, remembering angry exchanges or emotions left unexpressed. Help by giving them the opportunity to pour all this out.

This stage may be overtaken by bouts of intense sadness, manifested by silence and withdrawal from family and friends and by frequent outbursts of tears. Don't let Mum or Dad's physical needs be overlooked when they are feeling so alone and sorry for themselves.

Time heals to an extent, and the strong emotional responses, the pain, sadness and depression, diminish so that life becomes more bearable. With this revival comes an acceptance that is more a 'letting be' than a 'letting go'.

Of course, an Ofcap's role varies hugely, depending on your parent's age and state of health and the closeness or otherwise of the relationship between the two of you. It is possible your Mum or Dad has been widowed for many years, like May, whose situation we will learn about later. In that case, you may simply have a supportive role, similar to that of a loyal, trustworthy friend, so that you are there – certainly at the end of a phone but hopefully more often in person – to enjoy shared experiences. It is later, when Mum or Dad's needs increase, perhaps through the onset of illness or with advancing age, that the emphasis alters and you become a fully fledged Ofcap.

Invariably, you'll find you need to be resourceful, rather as you may have been with your children when they were toddlers. Filling a blank day with a walk and a few trips to the washing line stood you in good stead when caring for a two year old, so why not do the same with Mum or Dad? It's company and the closeness of loved ones that they crave, not wing-walking lessons.

Although, it has to be said, I wouldn't put a spot of wing-walking past my Mother, whose highly developed sense of fun and adventure is both a challenge and a delight. On a trip to Tate Britain, which involved a long journey by coach, tube and taxi, she showed more interest in going for a ride over London in an airship, which she spotted as it drifted over the Thames, than she did in the exhibition we were headed for. She was 79 at the time. The following year, to mark her 80th birthday, my sister and I flew her to Venice for the day and she was at the top of the campanile when the bells suddenly rang out in a mad cacophony that sent us scuttling into a corner, our hands ineffectually over our ears. We like to think the bells were for the birthday girl, but it's possible they were tolling the hour.

Such a memorable excursion took considerable planning, so if you fancy doing something similar, don't expect it to be one of those impetuous, jolly escapades dreamed up one weekend and executed the next. This one required months of groundwork once the seed had been sown, and then there was the Great Passport Adventure to be lived through. "It's all right, I've got a passport," said Mum, confidently. It's true, she had: last used in 1959 and bearing the portrait of someone looking like a very much younger version of me. The Adventure took many twists and turns along the way, including having to start all over again – twice. It also took immense patience on the part of the man at the post office and the entire staff of the camera shop where the nerve-jangling photo shoot took place.

Briefly, if you're faced with getting Mum or Dad a new passport, quit your job, set aside at least a year of your life, take anger management lessons, and for heaven's sake make sure the witnesses know how to spell your parent's name (Mistake No.1) and they don't use a fountain pen (Mistake No.2). After that, with the beastly thing in your hot hand (not at large in you-know-who's gargantuan handbag or the inside pocket of Dad's jacket-on-the-back-of-the-chair) the hanging around at the airport is a holiday in itself.

Many new widows and widowers take life by the scruff of the neck and get on with living it, despite their grief. After years of caring for an ailing partner, one 69 year old widow packed her bags and set off to China, via the Trans-Siberian Express. It was Canada the next year, then New Zealand. Her Ofcap, feeling somewhat abandoned, has never had a chance to get stuck in to her new role but is kept busy all the same – compiling a post-card collection.

Travel is one of those things that can be accomplished relatively easily as a couple but which can seem impossibly daunting alone. But it's not always a simple matter of confidence, as Ofcaps may find. Some have been alarmed to learn that Mum refuses to come and stay once she's alone.

Promises of being spoilt in the company of her family have no effect. If it's the train that's worrying you, we'll come and get you, they reassure her. Still there comes the adamant refusal.

Eventually, after careful questioning, the concerned Ofcaps discover the reason. Mum won't budge from home because she doesn't want to enjoy herself. She really means it when she says she would feel guilty having fun with the family when her husband wasn't with her.

The guilt won't stay with her for ever, so while Mum's working through her feelings don't make her feel bad about saying no. Be patient and include her in day trips, by all means, but don't expect her to come and play her old role in Happy Families until she's ready.

For all the open weepers, the silent sufferers and the ones who refuse to accept the loss, there are just as many who subconsciously show their feelings in other ways, perhaps through a determination to honour their late partner. One man found therapeutic distraction in tracing and compiling his late wife's family tree. He found solace in an activity that was not only fascinating and absorbing but that maintained a link with her and her memory. Importantly, he didn't feel guilty, either, about being so enjoyably occupied.

As our parents get older they naturally like to continue to be thought of as useful members of the human race. Don't consign them to some geriatric wasteland just because they no longer wear a suit to work each day or they've given up driving. Use their fund of knowledge, consult them, seek their advice, run ideas past them, tap their life skills and you will undoubtedly be very pleasantly surprised. Do what you can to encourage them to use their time and energies for the benefit of others beyond the family as well, which has the advantage of extending their horizons and, in turn, increasing their self-worth.

My Dad, possessor of an encyclopaedic knowledge but in his later years confined to the house, was my personal Encyclopaedia Britannica on the end of a telephone line. He was also my Dictionary of National Biography and my spellchecker, all utterly invaluable to me. Mum, once widowed and moved near me and my sister, has quickly made herself useful in many ways – as a church cleaner, a museum guide, a charity bookstall helper, and as one of a trained team of conservators cleaning and preserving old books. It simply never occurs to her to say "No, I can't." Her keep-fit class gets squeezed in to the week's commitments, too, and she wisely keeps an engagement calendar so she knows where she's meant to be going and when. Not surprisingly, her grandchildren adore her lively company – when they can find her in.

Keeping occupied needn't all be altruistic. There's one 72 year old man who, two years after losing his wife, decided to do what he'd always wanted to do before he got too old. Consequently, he is now a proud season ticket holder at the Stoop and goes to watch every Harlequins home match. He's also a keen follower of the England rugby team and is a regular at Twickenham. His son says it's given him a wonderful new purpose in his life and gives them plenty to talk about when they get together.

Contrast this with the desperately grieving widow who, more than three years after the sudden death of her husband, spurns all offers of help, ignores all advice, turns her back on her friends and neighbours and makes impossible demands on her son and daughter. She's called Anthea and there'll be more about her later in the book. One of her difficulties is a deep rooted depression, an ailment not uncommon among the bereaved. Treatment invariably involves taking antidepressants, but these have no effect on the underlying grief. If the sufferer does not seek treatment for depression it makes it very difficult to grieve effectively.

There is a difference between depression and grief. Someone can grieve without being depressed, even though some of the feelings are much the same.

However, about a third of bereaved people also have a depressive illness after a month or so, and 15 per cent are still depressed a year later.

Symptoms that can indicate a bereaved person is also depressed include:

- Feelings of helplessness, worthlessness and guilt
- Prolonged or severe inability to work, socialise or enjoy a leisure activity
- Restlessness, difficulty concentrating, remembering and making decisions
- Insomnia, early morning awakening, or oversleeping
- Lying in bed doing nothing all day

It is ironic that a number of those symptoms put one in mind of the average teenager. But that must be where the similarity ends. The two, the bereaved and the teenager, could not merit equal treatment. It wouldn't be any good a frustrated Ofcap shouting and threatening loss of privileges to an aged parent, even if it's always worth a try with a teenager.

Overt emotional reaction to grief can last as long as a year (with the occasional exception, such as Anthea), but the average is about six months. Significant birthdays, anniversary dates and Christmas may bring about a resurgence of the symptoms, so Ofcaps need to be sensitive to these times and perhaps lend a hand in the planning of ways to mark them.

In the case of my own Mum, she likes to go and have a 'chat' with Dad at his memorial stone on or around his birthday. The timing tends to be dictated more by the weather than by the actual date, because a 250 mile round trip is best done when the sun is shining to lift the spirits.

Kid gloves needn't be required indefinitely when dealing with someone who has been widowed. Tea and sympathy, yes without a doubt, but there will come a time, maybe three years or so down the line, when what is popularly termed 'closure' can be achieved and a different, less troubled, phase of widowhood embarked upon.

Anthea, let us hope, is an exception. At the other extreme is Joan, who was widowed in her mid-50s when her husband died of a heart attack. She recovered remarkably well from the shock and from the turbulence of finding herself homeless, as the house had been tied to her husband's job as a parish priest. She proved herself to be, in her daughter Helen's words, "a very brave and gutsy widow", a strong character who showed tremendous kindness to her family and to the people in the village where she settled. She was, Helen says, a loved and valued member of the community and a wonderful Mum. She had also shown immense strength and compassion when Helen's own husband died, offering comfort and practical support, always at just the right times. Such sensitivity seems hard to equate with the cantankerous, difficult, demanding woman Joan was to become in later years, of which more will be revealed.

Beverley became an Ofcap to her father, Bill, a retired store-man living in a bungalow a couple of miles from her home in Hampshire, when her mother died after many years of being an invalid. Bill had proved to be a selfless and kind carer to his wife, so he was happy to be given the chance to look after his youngest grandchild when Beverley went back to full time work. "Dad was brilliant and totally reliable," she says. "It was wonderful to see the relationship grow between him and Becky and it really helped him through his grief over losing Mum. It gave him a purpose in his life again."How this developed will be explored later in the book.

Having a highlight and a purpose in each day is important to those whose newly solo lives lack variety. Loneliness, isolation, a dull routine and dreary sameness are all stultifying for those who have always enjoyed sharing experiences. Suddenly to be on your own, with the purpose for getting up each day no longer there and no eager ear waiting to listen to your account of the day, is hard to get accustomed to and harder still to live with indefinitely.

Norah found a solution to this when she was widowed: she became a frequent, and not always welcome, caller at her daughter's home. As an Ofcap, daughter Sally couldn't be entirely resentful and indeed did her utmost to be welcoming and sensitive, but, as she says "it became particularly wearing after a day's work to be called on by Mum, anxious to tell me what she'd watched on TV that afternoon." Norah's home was only a few steps away from Sally's, so it was only too easy for the 'popping in' to become a habit. It turned from an irritation into a problem once Norah started carping about Sally's handling of her teenage daughters, as we'll see in the next chapter.

While there are many different ways of coping with the emotional trauma of bereavement, there are precious few when it comes to practical matters. The simplest answer to the mysteries of life that afflict the newly widowed is probably just to send out a call for help. If an out-of-reach light bulb in the hall needs changing, a strip light tube in the kitchen has just gone pop, the kitchen sink is blocked, the loo won't flush and there's a slate off the roof, no-one wants their live-alone Mum to shin up a ladder or down a drain. Encourage her to make use of that list of useful numbers you've left for her by the telephone – but perhaps it's best if you're on hand to administer first aid for shock when the plumber's bill arrives.

It isn't really the done thing for her to put in an SOS call when she wants to change channels on the television, though. Maybe she's spent six months watching *attheraces* on Channel 4 and is curious to know if there are any other programmes. After all, when her husband was alive they used to watch quite a variety of programmes. He seemed to find them by using that thing he called the zapper that he always had by his side.

Teaching someone over the age of about 50 how to use a TV remote control is like trying to explain the periodic table to a toddler. But where there's a will there's a way, and if the alternative is to spend more confused hours *attheraces* with the jolly team from Channel 4, then mastering that hostile zapper suddenly seems a good idea.

When she was left a widow, ever-practical May had to show yet more strength of character. Her situation was that she lived in a large house miles from anywhere in Norfolk, her two sons and their families were two hours' journey away in different directions, and she had a choice: she could either sink or swim. She swam, magnificently and proudly, with her head held high. Her sons, Douglas and Hugh, have the greatest respect for how she coped. "She will always be something of a heroine in our eyes," says Douglas. "Not an ounce of self-pity, not a whimper of complaint. She missed Father a hell of a lot and she'd always enjoy reminiscing, especially as the years went on, but she never dwelt on what might have been. She was a widow: trust her, she would cope."

May's sort of coping included some impressive DIY plumbing repairs and 200 metres of hedge-laying along one side of the paddock next to the house. She turned her kitchen into a production line for a stall she ran with a friend at the Country Market and for relaxation she learned to play the French horn. Every summer she continued the family tradition of hosting the family holiday on the Broads. On her own and in her mid-60s, May grasped all the nettles Fate had flung at her and simply did what had to be done to get on with life. Only many years later did the stings begin to hurt, but as Ofcaps, Douglas and Hugh admit they had it pretty easy in the early days.

Our sixth and final Ofcap is Jenny, wife, mother of two sons, aged 11 and 16, full time advertising executive with a newspaper group, and, at the time she took on responsibility for her father, Jack, still deeply upset by the loss of her mother. To make matters worse, Jack treated Jenny like dirt. In spite of this, Jenny feels guilty to this day that she doesn't love him. She loved her mother very much and is appalled by the feelings she sometimes has when she wishes it had been her father who had died and not her mother.

CHAPTER 2

Your place or mine?

It's one thing trying cope with the distress of being widowed or becoming ill and dependent but quite another when the talk turns to moving house: so much to think about, so many pros and cons to weigh up, and so much depending on the decision.

If you are a far-flung Ofcap in this situation, whether you dress up the possibilities in fancy talk involving 'getting out from that rut', or you stress the financial benefits (assuming there are some), or the joy of meeting like-minded people in a home, your Mum or Dad is almost certainly going to resist. And wouldn't you?

The family home, undoubtedly steeped in memories and with friendly whispers in every corner, given up for four new walls in alien territory? Thanks, but no.

So you don't push it, mindful that at this time it's best to go along with the natural desire for a quiet life. The prospect of Mum or Dad staying put even has its attractions. But the weight of responsibility does not go away. The initiative will almost inevitably lie with you – or with you and your siblings, Ofcaps all.

And that, it hardly needs to be said, is where more minefields lie. Which of you pushes hardest for the decision, which of you is best placed geographically, and which of you ultimately gets handed the sad-faced person who is bravely trying to start a new life? Of you and your siblings, whose burden is greatest and whose guilt is the most unbearable?

Thrashing out the mechanics between you is best done well in advance of any hint-dropping to Mum, otherwise there's a danger that the idea of moving might be grasped and agreed upon before you and the gang have even thought about where, when and how. Once the best destination and timing have been settled, you can continue your chatting-up ploys.

When you next dare to bring up the subject, you suggest tentatively to Mum that she thinks about it carefully. What you may like to say, or even scream, is: "Think about us having to make this long journey to visit you. If you came to live closer/next door/with us (delete where applicable, depending on your courage and circumstances), everyone's lives would be changed for the better – yours included."

That's what you'd like to say, but compassion and good sense prevail so you continue to drip-feed enticing titbits of information, such as: "It's incredible, but the developers have sold all but two of those luxury old people's bungalows near us. Fancy that – just two left!" And "Lucy says her dad has never had a second's regret since moving into a sheltered flat – and he's been able to take his dog with him."

Another thing you would like to try and impress upon Mum or Dad is the fact that moving house is going to be much more bearable at this stage, while all the choices can be discussed and while there is a chance they can be involved in things like where to put the bed and which curtains to take or leave. It's a shame to delay the decision until someone in authority peers over their bifocals and insists, threateningly, that a move should be made 'before it's too late'.

If the preferred option is to stay put, at least for the time being, then look for the positives in that. Being spared the upheaval, for a start, is a major plus for Mum or Dad, along with the significant considerations of staying in familiar surroundings among friends, knowing where everything is and how to get to it, like post office, library and shops, and not having to worry about getting rid of items such as furniture and pictures to which there is a sentimental attachment. In a new home, there may not be space for all the worldly goods, and rationalising belongings is not a task for the faint-hearted or weak-willed so it is best done when Mum or Dad is focused and determined.

If a move is on the cards but the choice of exactly where and into what has yet to be determined, be sure to cast a wide net and explore all possibilities. Bear in mind all eventualities, so that you're not faced with masterminding another move too soon after this one. In other words, think about possibly cutting out the sensible bungalow stage altogether and heading straight for sheltered living or a development that has care facilities if not on the spot then at least on call.

Sensible Ofcaps would need a lot convincing of the wisdom of Mum or Dad either staying on in the former family home or moving somewhere that needs a lot of upkeep if the only bonus is enough spare bedrooms for the grandchildren to come and stay. After the age of about 11, grandchildren tend to prefer sleepovers with their friends to sleeping in the next room to a snoring Granny.

Downsizing Mum or Dad's accommodation need not mean losing out on the chance of family visits. Some old people's flats complexes have guest suites that can be rented very reasonably, or there is bound to be a convenient B&B, guest house, hotel or even letting cottage. That way, everyone has their space and privacy but there is loads of scope for valuable quality time together.

Security is one of the most important features to look for wherever Mum or Dad is thinking of moving. Being on their own is going to make them feel vulnerable anyway, so ensure there are security devices on doors and windows and sensibly placed smoke alarms (and check the batteries regularly).

Jack's Story

Difficult Jack, Jenny's Dad, took matters into his own hands within a year of losing his wife. He put his village house on the market because he decided he wanted to live in a sheltered flat in the nearest town. Such enterprise might have been welcomed in anyone else, but with Jack it was different. The main problem was that he had never lifted a finger for himself before his wife, Sylvia, died. She had run everything. Jack therefore knew little about what made things tick and how matters like selling a house should be tackled.

This was the time, says Jenny, when it dawned on her just what a liability her father was. Instead of waiting until he had had at least an offer on the house, Jack started to get rid of things and he even let a house clearance specialist come in and remove numerous possessions, including ornaments and a number of personal and precious things that had belonged to Jenny's grandmother. She was dreadfully upset, but Jack didn't realise the significance of what he was doing.

"Dad had no sense of family," Jenny says. "It was always Mum who'd kept up with family news and who ensured family ties weren't broken. He didn't do anything. He wouldn't have seen anyone if Mum hadn't organised it. I was shocked to discover how hopeless he was, what little grasp he had on anything. Mum had covered up for him throughout the 50 years of their marriage."

Sadly, this is not uncommon. We all know about the cast-adrift women who haven't a clue how to pay a bill or renew the TV licence, but how many men do you know who can competently look after themselves? Exactly. Being a domestically challenged male – to the point of not even knowing how to make toast – may have a certain storybook appeal, but it quickly becomes exasperating if you're the Ofcap clearing up the debris. Take a tip from a still fit couple in their 70s who have devised a personal survival strategy by which he does the shopping and cooking for a month and she does all the bills and manages the household finances. That way, they hope they will be self-sufficient through widowhood and they are very thoughtfully ensuring their Ofcaps are spared an experience like Jenny's.

Within a year of Sylvia's death, Jack had moved out of the family home that held so many memories for Jenny, and even sold his car. Once in the town he had everything within easy reach, including the pub.

Cars can fall into the same category as TV remote controls if Mum is not of a particularly technical bent. Few women of that older generation are, as evidenced by the numerous occasions when that terrifying lack of spatial awareness allied with a complete inability to park a car, find the bonnet catch, operate a petrol pump and change out of fourth gear causes smarty-pants male motorists to slap their foreheads and say 'I might've known it would be a flipping granny at the wheel'.

Unless you are prepared for your Mum or Dad to continue running the risk of killing or maiming themselves or others on the roads, you have a duty to mankind to keep them away from the wheel once you perceive that their driving skills are deteriorating towards danger levels. Unfortunately, driving can hold an important symbolism in the parent-child relationship, not least because it represents freedom and independence. Take the car away and you take the status away. What's left is someone who can't get about easily any more – a dependant.

Hardly surprising, then, that one Dad whose Toad of Toad Hall tendencies behind the wheel caused his Ofcap to get him to agree to sell his car, went out and bought another after a fortnight of fury and foul temper.

Telling Mum outright that you consider she shouldn't go on driving because she's a danger to herself and a downright menace to all other drivers, not to mention unsuspecting pedestrians, falls into the category of being cruel to be kind. It worked with my Mum, who I think was quite relieved, if truth be told, that she no longer had the responsibility of that intractable beast in the garage.

It may not be that easy, though, and different, more cunning, tactics may need to be employed. Try the pleading of a loved and loving grandchild to influence Granny or Grandpa, and so avoid being labelled the 'bossy daughter' (on this occasion at least).

Norah's story

Norah had already moved by the time she was widowed. She and her husband, Ted, swapped one cathedral city for another – leaving Durham and settling near Worcester – to be near their only daughter, Sally. They wanted to support Sally, a widow and school headteacher, as she brought up her two girls.

The move worked well for Norah and Ted and they made their

own lives, relishing new surroundings and the chance to travel occasionally, while still being close at hand if Sally needed them. Ted enjoyed a new project, too, as he oversaw the building of a cottage in Sally's garden where he and Norah eventually moved, bringing the whole family even closer.

"It was great having Mum and Dad right there," says Sally. "We'd always got on well so there were never any problems, even though my younger daughter, Suzy, could occasionally cause some upsets with her disruptive behaviour. She's got fairly severe autism, so life's never been easy for her."

Only 18 months after Norah and Ted moved into the cottage in Sally's garden, Ted had a stroke and, while still in hospital, he suffered two more and died. The family's happy equilibrium was shattered.

"If Mum hadn't already been living next-door to me I would have persuaded her to move as soon as she felt able," says Sally. "It would have been the obvious thing to do, and I'm sure she'd have come. As it was, she didn't have to suffer that upheaval, so we were both lucky in that respect."

Having Norah next-door was not all unalloyed pleasure, however. Without Ted, the focus of her life inevitably shifted on to Sally and the girls, and that was when, from Sally's point of view, things started to get difficult.

"The situation became uneasy when Mum kept having little digs at me about how I was handling the girls. Beth must have been about 16 at the time and Suzy was 14. Beth's life was all mobile phones and friends and going out and socialising. Suzy's was different, very fraught, very tense and very much driven by how good or otherwise she happened to be feeling on any particular day.

"Mum found this hard to grasp. How could Beth be so hedonistic while her 'poor little Suzy' was suffering so much? I explained to Mum a thousand times that Suzy's concept of happiness and contentment was not the same as her sister's, but she wouldn't have it.

"She latched on to this and banged on about it time and time again, presumably getting years of built-up angst off her chest. Needless to say, it wasn't long before she was giving me advice on how to cope with Beth and Suzy, saying I ought to impose ridiculous things like a 9pm curfew on Beth so that Suzy wouldn't feel left out.

"Because I'm a widow myself I could understand some of the turmoil that Mum was suffering and how her emotions were probably getting the better of her, but I couldn't tolerate her interference in my upbringing of the girls. I wanted to tell her that my life was difficult enough without her picking holes in it. I also felt like saying to her that she'd only had one daughter and I'd had two and there's a big, big difference, especially when one of them has severe learning difficulties.

"We had some huge rows. As if it wasn't enough having two hormonal teenagers in my home, I now had a third force, pulling me in another direction and making me seethe with anger.

"I think Mum had always seen Beth and Suzy as lovely girls, polite and charming, because she had only been in their company when everyone was being pleasant to each other. But now that Mum was with them for hours at a time, on their own home territory, she was appalled by their normal teenage behaviour and wanted them to change back into those sweet girls she used to know.

"Deep down, I also suspect Mum didn't like the fact I worked. Not only did my job have an impact on the children, in that I'd always had to pay someone to do the ironing and to be there to get them their tea on the days they came home from school before me, but now, of course, it was keeping me away from her as well.

"She was interfering more and more in the lives of the three of us and was becoming increasingly dependent on me for company. She'd make disappointed noises if I ever had to explain that I'd be working late, or that I was going somewhere with one of my friends."

Cute grannies exist in storybooks but only occasionally in real life. Surprisingly often they can be cantankerous and difficult. For Ofcaps trapped in the middle of two warring generations it can be incredibly wearing. There's disapproval from above, disdain from below, but you have to draw out the best in both, deflecting Grandma's criticism of the younger generation and encouraging grandchildren to have respect for their elders. The trouble is, there is so much implied criticism of you in all the words that are flying about: your fault for having children like that, your fault for having a parent like that.

You can only aim to reach a situation of compromise with yourself, knowing you can't win. Your only hope is to bite your tongue and count to 10. And vow that one day you will be a cute granny with a broad mind, a short memory and deep pockets.

Norah's intrusiveness saddened Sally because it was in such contrast to how their juxtaposed lives had been when both her parents lived in the garden cottage. Then, there had been undemanding coexistence, each household respecting the other's independence.

"It was so ideal I suppose I might have known it wouldn't – or couldn't – last," says Sally. "When Mum took to criticising Beth's choice of underwear, presumably because she'd been scrutinising some of her flimsy bras and thongs on the washing line, I just about flipped. She objected to Beth's limpet-like hold on her mobile phone, too. And she tried to correct her every time she spoke, even suggesting she should take elocution lessons. I ask you! No wonder Beth tried to keep out of her way.

"As for her 'poor little Suzy' – Mum suggested I should think about moving her to a different school as she didn't seem to be making any progress. What progress do you expect the child to make, my mind bellowed at her, while my face smiled and replied sweetly that I'd think about it.

"Because Mum had lost her confidence since Dad died I really couldn't blast her out and expect her to mind her own business. Her world had shrunk to this size, to her and the three of us, and if I excluded her she'd have no-one else. So I kept my temper and explained to her that I actually enjoyed my work, that my daughters were not evil monsters and that the world would go on turning if I left the breakfast washing-up until we were all home in the evening.

"It was a shame she resented my job. I am certain she disapproved of the fact I worked, because she had never had to. She'd been the archetypal stay-at-home housewife and mother whereas I have a career. If only she'd taken the time and trouble to understand what I did she might have felt differently. Without Dad there any more she didn't seem to know the questions to ask."

Helen's story

Helen had always promised her mother that she would do whatever it took to keep her in her own home, even when it became necessary for her to have round-the-clock care. Joan was housebound for the last three years of her life, but lived to be 90, buoyed by a deep religious faith, an indomitable spirit and a dedicated team of carers. The routine that ran Joan's life was orchestrated by Helen from her home 250 miles away in London.

Dutiful, devoted and loving Helen played a part in that routine herself when she took over the caring role for a weekend every fortnight, travelling to the corner of south-west Wales for what she describes as "two punishing days of physical and mental torment".

"At the end of my visit I would be utterly incapable of driving 250 miles home again because I was so exhausted," Helen says. "Mum brought me to my knees and absolutely drained me of every ounce of energy. The most I could manage of the home-ward journey on a Sunday night was 60 miles and then I'd stop at a B&B and leave for work in London at the crack of dawn next morning."

Being in the house with her mother, says Helen, was "a complete and utter nightmare. She had become completely impossible." But, come hell, high water and massive care bills, Helen kept her promise to Joan.

May's story

Plucky and capable May, hedge-layer extraordinaire and holiday hostess for her sons and their families, stayed on in the big house until Douglas and Hugh put forward a proposal that they had long thought would be the way forward for when Mother became a bit doddery to be living on her own. But long before then, May had sprung a bit of a surprise on the family.

Her daughter-in-law, Carol, who is married to Douglas, says the "interesting episode" started about five years after May had been widowed, when she was in her late 60s. "She announced to us, in a very matter-of-fact way, that she was going to start going out more in the hope of meeting a new partner. We were all flabbergasted – not because of what she wanted to do, but because she'd told us. I imagine it was to spare our feelings if we heard about it from anyone else.

"Douglas and Hugh were more surprised than upset that she could think about bringing someone new into her life – or all of our lives, because it would have a big effect on the grand-children, too.

"I couldn't help wondering what Douglas's father would have thought. Then we began to see it from May's point of view, you know – the prospect of years more on her own, being fun and lively and having so much to offer – and we became more rec-onciled to the idea."

Once May had embarked on her mission it took on a different meaning for all the family. At first it was treated lightly, says Douglas. Then, when the first man was introduced to the fam-ily one summer holiday, it all became more serious. "I liked him," Douglas says, "but it wasn't until later that the thought crossed my mind that he might become my stepfather. That idea took some getting used to.

"As things turned out, he was a key part of Mum's life for several years until he died, but they were never more than social partners – good, reliable friends, who enjoyed going out occasionally together. We were totally comfortable with the arrangement because it gave both their lives an extra dimension."

It can be terribly difficult meeting new people and making friends when you're no longer young and you're on your own. It is not just that the opportunities are fewer, either. It is the lack of a partner, that dear old familiar who was always at your side, that makes it so hard because with two there is a certain confidence. When it's just one, there's uncertainty and diffidence.

You need to be aware of this when you cheerily encourage your now single parent to join in with some activity or another. One 76 year old showed amazing grit when, during her first Christmas as a widow, she volunteered to help out at the local residential home. Her Ofcaps were proud of her for finding such a positive way of overcoming her loneliness. But it didn't go as well as it might, through nobody's fault. One of her helpful duties was to sit and chat with some of the old people, which was fine. But then the dance music started up and she was asked if she'd take one of her charges for a waltz across the floor. This was nearly her undoing, because the last person she had held in her arms was her beloved husband.

Time, as we know, is a great healer, so beware of pushing the 'be sociable' button too hard too soon.

Douglas and Hugh's plan for the removal of May, by now aged 88, from the house where she had lived for more than 60 years, was fairly drastic. She would move into a flat in a 'very sheltered living' complex about three miles away from them. What did she think of that? Absolutely fine, thank you, she replied, and when do we start?

"Mum never put up any resistance to what, in effect, was a vast upheaval at a late stage of her life," says Douglas. "She really was terrific. Of course, we made it as stress free as possible for her, so that she didn't have to get involved in any of the mechanics of the house move or the sale, just sign bits of paper."

Hugh, May's elder son, was by this time divorced and living in the south of France. Like Douglas, he was recently retired so they both had time to organise what they referred to as the EOM, the Extraction of Mother. Nevertheless, it was Douglas who masterminded it all and who continued to be the driving force.

It is a remarkable fact that nowadays old people move more times in their last five years than at any previous period in their lives. The shuffle from long-time family home to old people's bungalow, to hospital, to nursing home, to hospice, is a familiar one, and the pass-the-parcel from one hospital ward to another perhaps even more so.

A consultant physician with special responsibility for the elderly regrets the situation. "None of us wants to see people moved," he says. "In this hospital (in the south of England) at the moment it is appalling how many times elderly people have to be moved from ward to ward. We all recognise it makes for poor care for the patient, they have to stay in hospital longer, are more liable to pick up infections and it is not satisfying for the staff, having a continual succession of different patients to look after."

Bill's story

All the family were consulted before Beverley asked her widowed father, Bill, if he'd like to come and live with them five years ago. With the two older children having moved out and only herself, her husband Alec and younger daughter Becky left in the large, four-bedroom house, it seemed a good idea to relieve Bill of the responsibility and burden of looking after himself and to put him safely under their roof. But first of all, everyone needed to be on side.

Becky, aged 11 at the time, was very excited because she and her grandpa had formed such a close bond during the time they'd spent together when she was little. As her part time childminder in those days, Bill had proved to be compassionate and reliable – qualities which Beverley was sure would make him an easy-going house-sharer.

Bill thought he'd been coping well on his own but, although he was in generally good health, his mobility was becoming more and more of a problem. A hip replacement operation 15 years earlier had been only a partial success because a chronic infection deep in the bone had left him in constant pain, despite a subsequent operation to try and clear it. He had had two falls, too, the more recent when he was outside his bungalow early on a cold winter morning. He lay helpless for three hours before he was found and Beverley was concerned about his vulnerability.

With the family and Bill in agreement that the move would be a good idea, a date was set. Everyone, for their own different reasons, was happy at the prospect. Bill sold his bungalow, gave Beverley, his only child, a lump sum and packed his bags to start a new life, at the age of 79, in the family's detached house in a quiet close. There was an armchair and a television in his bedroom and space to put all his things.

"At first I was excited and pleased to have Dad with us," says Beverley. "It seemed to work well and everything was just how I'd imagined it would be."

But what nobody could have imagined was how the happy domestic situation would, over time, turn so sour.

One of the main considerations for both sides faced with the prospect of Mum or Dad moving in is 'how will we all get on together?' The obvious answer is 'Fine. We're all related, we all love each other, we get on well, there shouldn't be a problem.' Because it will have been many years since you were under the same roof for any length of time, everyone will have developed their daily routines which, without anyone realising, have become life props.

Check out these niggling habits:

1 Clearing the throat and/or little coughs
2 Constant sniffing
3 Using too much loo roll
4 TV constantly on at high volume
5 Fussing over trivia and detail

Any of the above, plus any number of others, which, as we all know, could run into millions, can quickly magnify into intolerable irritations out of all proportion.

Under these circumstances it is well to heed this adaptation of a popular slogan: 'Granny is for life, not just for Christmas'. Think ahead to how you are all going to feel when, this time, she doesn't pack her case and go home after a fortnight. Your home is now her home.

Discuss what expectations you all have about any proposed home-sharing, whether it's upstairs, downstairs or in a granny annexe, and don't allow anyone to commit themselves until all potential problem areas have been identified and solved. This is a time for being honest and upfront, not for being a martyr.

Anthea's story

When Anthea's husband died she was poleaxed. He'd always done everything round the house, made all the decisions and just about done her thinking for her. Left alone, she seemed hardly capable of breathing unaided. Bob, her son, despaired. "Her GP told me she'd need a lot of careful handling, plenty of attention and probably some counselling. We gave her the lot, and more, but she barely responded.

"It was awful to see her decline so badly, but she just didn't seem to want to live. Nothing we did made any difference. It was as though she was shrivelling up into a little ball waiting to die.

"Of course we felt sorry for her, but at the same time we feared for her sanity – and for our own. We also couldn't bear to think about the future. We just pinned our hopes on a softly-softly approach and a gradual turning round, away from bleakness into some kind of normality."

Bob and his sister, Kate, say they felt so guilty about not being able to be with her as much as they felt she needed them that they started telephoning every day, one of them at lunchtime, the other in the early evening. It soon became a dreadful chore, punctuating their busy lives, but they knew that once they'd got into the routine there was no easy way out. Stopping the phone calls, or even reducing them, would, they were sure, increase Anthea's insecurity because she often told them how much she enjoyed the daily chats.

Anthea's house had been on the market at the time of her husband's death. Their plan had been to move out of rural Hertfordshire and nearer Bob and Kate and their families in London. Against her Ofcaps' advice, the new widow went ahead with the sale of the house which had so many happy memories. But then, instead of making the planned move, she decided to stay in the same village, choosing to buy a thatched cottage with four bedrooms and an unnecessarily large garden.

"It was a case of out of the frying pan and into the fire," Bob says. "Nothing would deflect her from this completely insane, irrational step. And, of course, as soon as she had made the move, she regretted it.

"She used to say she could hear Dad talking to her in the old house, but there was just an echoing silence in the new one. It was the worst thing she could ever have done."

Faced with such intractability in their Mother, Bob and Kate did all they possibly could to influence her into making what they could see was the right decision. They failed. She would not listen and went her own way. In a situation like this, you can only give your best advice – and, of course, resist the temptation later to say 'I told you so'.

Anthea's distress manifested itself in a number of ways, most notably in a withdrawal into a deep trough of depression. Her apathy even extended to her grandchildren in whom she now showed little interest, visiting them only once in London – and that was because protocol demanded she attend the christening of the new baby.

"There's no reason for me to go on living," she would say flatly to anyone brave enough to ask her how she was getting on.

Bob reckons it was hard to argue with her on that fact, despite the valiant efforts he and his sister made for more than two years. "We tried to involve her in our lives as much as possible," he says, "but she made it clear we were wasting our time. She alienated most of her friends, and those who remained in touch did so only through a sense of duty.

"It was tragic. She would just sit staring at photographs of Dad most of the time. The whole house was full of them so he was all around her.

"My sister and I arranged for Mum to have counselling when we realised she wasn't making any progress. It made a difference, if only because it enabled Mum to moan 'officially', but after about 18 months I think the poor counsellor was on the verge of a nervous breakdown. We could hardly blame her."

The biggest stumbling block in trying to help with counselling is attitude. Older people do not respond happily to the idea of sharing innermost thoughts or intimate details with someone else – whether that someone is a close family member or a complete stranger.

Some Age Concern branches offer counselling as one of their services, but it tends not to be readily seized upon as a useful lifeline by those who could most benefit from it. "It's very much an attitude of their age – they're just not comfortable with the idea," a voluntary trained counsellor says. "They don't open up, so they keep their troubles to themselves. It's a shame, because counselling can definitely help."

Distraction can be therapeutic, too, so try to encourage a troubled, grieving Mum to make a scrapbook of her memories. Assure her that the whole family would like it, as a source of interest and pleasure, but also as a tribute to Dad. Levels of motivation will be at zero, so don't expect her to whip out the scissors and glue and create something worthy of a Blue Peter badge all on her own. Do it with her, then you both get all sorts of benefits, not least the pleasure of each other's company.

As an incentive, keep focused on the best spin-off you could hope for: that Mum will become so heartily sick of dwelling on the past that she'll get to the end of the scrapbook project as quickly as possible, lock it away in a cupboard, and start looking the world in the face again.

Anthea's helplessness and total lack of motivation took their toll on her family's sympathy. They found it difficult to persist in their efforts to buoy up her spirits when they got nothing in return. "To be honest," says Bob, the elder Ofcap, "it was as much as my sister and I could do to carry on with our daily phone calls, let alone go and see Mum regularly. I often stayed overnight and by lunchtime the next day I would be almost screaming to escape."

Both the Ofcaps felt Anthea would be better off not living on her own, but perhaps living with one of them. Neither felt they could cope with her for longer than a month, but they thought it might break the spell she seemed to be under. Anthea was adamant she wasn't going to move, insisting she had all she needed around her, including the village hall, where she hadn't been for at least five years, and the village shop, from where she consistently returned without any of the things on her shopping list. Friends were important to her, too, she told Bob and Kate. Yet no friends or neighbours had been to call since the early days of her widowhood.

While they didn't want to unsettle Anthea and damage her already low morale, Bob and Kate were anxious that any change in their mother's life shouldn't come about through an accident. They wanted it to be planned and executed painlessly, but in the meantime, her independence was obviously important to her and they agreed they would maintain that for as long as possible.

CHAPTER 3

Decline and fall

Bodies aren't made to last for ever. There comes a time when bits deteriorate or pack up altogether and, however much we may curse, and however clever surgeons may be, they refuse to go back together again satisfactorily. If none of this has happened by the time you've notched up threescore years and 10, then you're not only lucky but probably in the minority as well.

Our parents, whom we can recall – if only dimly – kicking a football about or running alongside a pony while we bounced astride it and whooped with joy, are now distinctly wrinkly and crumbly round the edges. Zipping up and down a soccer pitch is something they only do in their dreams, when the call is made to the Cup Final crowd and out steps Grandpa, aged 26, all rippling thigh muscles and Georgie Best hair, to lead his team to glory.

And what a lot of dreaming goes on. Older people seem to spend a great deal of time asleep. Many nod off at odd times of the day because they either sleep badly at night or wake ridiculously early, but most take daytime naps as a matter of routine, slotting in at least 40 winks after lunch, with at least a couple more rounds before bedtime.

Unreliable bodies have a lot to answer for as they inflict hardship and pain and sadness on the undeserving and, in many cases, the unsuspecting. Just when a chap least deserves to be strapped into a straitjacket, he's told he's got late onset diabetes and must follow a strict diet for the rest of his life. Or some lithe, fit 70 year old, a blameless paragon of clean living, is told she has dangerously high cholesterol and a bad dose of gout.

The older one gets the more difficult it is to deflect these unkind slaps in the face. Where a parent is concerned, the greatest need is for emotional and physical support. Leave diagnoses and treatment to the experts, but Ofcaps need to be there for the sharing of anger or distress at bad news, and prepared to help with acquiring whatever is needed in the way of special foods or equipment, be willing to fetch and carry, visit, keep company with and generally comfort someone you love who is entering another stage of their lives. This time it could be frightening and they need you badly.

A healthy lifestyle, based on a good diet and a sensible amount of exercise, is the obvious ideal. How to achieve this when you're dealing with someone who was brought up on Spam sandwiches washed down with cups of sweet, milky tea, and an occasional treat of fish and chips, is not easy. All the leaflets, all the homilies, all the good-sense TV programmes in the world aren't going to change an older person's bad habits overnight.

Your only hope, if you are faced with stubborn indifference to the notion of eating sensibly, is to persuade Mum or Dad to come shopping with you and open their eyes to some of the alternatives. If they can't be bothered to get out pots and pans to cook – and that is surprisingly common among people living on their own, of whatever age – then they might be interested in bunging everything into a slow cooker, like my Mum does. Whole meals emerge from this wonderful contraption, thanks to the judicious placing of foil containers, one with the main course, one with pudding. Sliced beef, potatoes, runner beans and gravy, followed by a baked apple, is many people's idea of a delicious lunch, and for a hungry octogenarian who has been up since dawn it's a fine reward for a little forward planning and ingenuity.

Slow cookers have three important advantages:

1   They create virtually no smell
2   They cause very little washing-up
3   They are safe to use

And if you're looking for more, consider these:

4   No gas
5   No flames
6   No hot plates to leave on

Who could ask for a simpler solution to a worrying problem?

As for an older person's exercise, this is obviously dictated by their mobility or lack of it. Hopefully, they'll want to get out and about, but it's when they can't, or won't, that other strategies need to be considered for their own good.

There are all manner of sporting and leisure initiatives at a local level, of which some, such as gentle yoga or swimming, with classes specifically for older people, may appeal. If Mum or Dad would benefit from a boost in the fitness of their body and mind, suggest they join a t'ai chi class, which strengthens the important core muscles, improves breathing and imparts a sense of well-being. It can be practised at home, too, and no equipment is needed. Better still, learn t'ai chi with them and appreciate what it can do for you, too.

General health issues need to be monitored by Ofcaps. If Mum or Dad is on a small cocktail of medication make sure it is reviewed regularly, either by their GP or a pharmacist, to ensure they are getting the most benefit from it all. Be aware that over 65s are entitled to:

- Free immunisations against flu and pneumonia
- Free sight tests
- Free prescriptions

Feet and teeth (or maybe it's just gums in some cases) should be kept in good working order or they can let their owner down, painfully.

If you're not sure what services, such as chiropody or physiotherapy, are available, ask at their GP's surgery or contact their local Age Concern (Helpline: 0800 731 4931 **www.ageconcern.org.uk**). The idea of using complementary therapies, which can be so beneficial to bodies and lift the spirits, ought to be run past the GP first.

Anthea's story

For some time, probably more than a year, Bob and Kate had each noticed that, alongside her apathy, Anthea had been forgetful, having difficulty remembering names of things and people. She also seemed to be having trouble using the washing machine, appearing baffled by what she had hitherto operated with ease.

Kate decided the best way of finding out the extent of the problems was to take a week off work to go and stay with her Mother so she could assess her more closely on a daily basis. She quite quickly became alarmed by what she found. "It was obvious that Mum had been covering up rather well for what had probably been ages and ages," she says. "Maybe even Dad had covered up for her while he was still alive, but now she was getting worse and she couldn't do anything about it so she was being exposed. Poor Mum was struggling so much we hardly needed to say what was in our minds – that she was showing signs of dementia."

It is important to know the symptoms of dementia because Ofcaps sometimes blame their parent rather than the illness and they get annoyed and angry with them. The person with dementia doesn't know this is happening; they just know they aren't functioning as well as they used to, with a marked lack of self-esteem as an almost inevitable consequence.

One of the early symptoms is perceived as apathy. As a specialist in dementia explains:"The person knows she's not doing things properly so she doesn't do them at all. Her daughter may notice that she's lost interest in knitting the children's jumpers this year when the real reason she's not knitting them is that she's frightened of making a mistake.

"She opts out of situations that she would normally cope with and interests and enthusiasms that she previously had go by the board. She can't quite get a grip, so she doesn't do any of the things any more. She protects herself by withdrawing, then sometimes by going into denial. 'No it's not me, it's not my fault – I haven't lost my pension book, you've lost it.' So she's projecting her anxiety and mistakes on to somebody else.

"Deep down, someone with dementia becomes more and more frightened. People respond to fear in different ways. It's a coping mechanism. Denial in dementia is not a negative thing, it's a way of covering up the inevitable and it's their way of living with it. One of the hardest things to cope with in dementia is the fact that the personality is destroyed and what you're left with is a different person."

Incidents of forgetfulness, which Anthea's Ofcaps had put down to 'Mum's dottiness' in the previous year or so, included missing two appointments with the chiropodist and turning up at 6.30am one morning for an 11am appointment with the hairdresser. They'd pulled her leg about her eccentricity and encouraged her to keep a more careful note of what she was meant to be doing each day.

Bob confided in his sister that he'd noticed Anthea seemed increasingly remote, as if she was struggling with her own world. Anthea denied there was a problem of any sort and refused to see her GP when Kate suggested it, insisting he wouldn't want to be bothered by someone who wasn't ill. Kate was so concerned for her by this time that she asked Bob to join her at their mother's house and arranged for the doctor to call.

"It may have been devious of me," she says, "but it was the only thing I could think of doing. The doctor spent a little time with Anthea on her own in the sitting-room. He stopped in the hallway on his way out and told Bob and me that he was almost certain it was Alzheimer's. He handed Bob the prescription for Aricept and advised him to contact the Alzheimer's Society. That was it. Bob and I stared at each other in despair. We were just being left to cope."

The initial diagnosis is like a death, according to a specialist in Alzheimer's. There are two deaths that the carer has to get through: the death of the person who was in full flight and the final death. The initial death is the harder one.

Dementia is a broad term which means a progressive loss in a person's ability to remember, to think and to reason. All types of dementia are physical illnesses, not mental illnesses.

About three-quarters of a million people in the UK have dementia, of whom half a million have Alzheimer's, a disease that destroys brain cells through changes in the chemistry and structure of the brain.

With the diagnosis of Alzheimer's confirming their fears about their mother, Bob and Kate knew there would come a time when she would be more confused, more vulnerable and her life would be in more danger, especially if she started wandering.

"We were entering a world of which we knew virtually nothing," Kate says, "but both Bob and I were aware, from what little we'd gleaned about Alzheimer's, that it was better for her to be kept in her own home, in familiar surroundings, for as long as possible."

The average duration of a dementia is about 12 years, although it may have been going on for some time before it is properly diagnosed. It used to be about seven or eight years but it now tends to be recognised earlier and there are several drugs available. An early diagnosis can make a significant difference, provided the right drugs are given, and symptoms can sometimes be arrested for a year or more.

There is no evidence that you can slow down the progress of Alzheimer's by doing mind exercises but by meeting with people and sharing experiences, the depression associated with dementia can be slightly lifted. A better self-image and better self-esteem enable people with dementia to function better.

Having dementia is a stroke of fate, unless it runs in the family genes. Over the age of 80 there's a one in five chance of dementia, and over the age of 90 the chance increases to one in two. What price a happy old age?

Jack's story

Jack had always drunk too much but his problem grew acute once he moved into sheltered accommodation in town, where he quickly became a regular in the pub that was nearest his flat. "Dad was like a child let loose in a sweet shop," says Jenny. "In fact he was childlike in many ways because he seemed not to be responsible for himself."

Every lunchtime and evening he drank heavily – always whisky – and would buy drinks for other people in the pub. Jenny is sure they took advantage of him. Among the problems caused by his drunkenness were several falls and an incident when he set his cooker on fire.

Jack's stubborn helplessness is not untypical of a man in his position. Now aged 76, he was only 72 when he was widowed just a little while after he had finally stopped working. He had been a train driver in Yorkshire and on retirement he became caretaker of the school at the end of the road, which Jenny and her sister had attended. Five years of that were followed by a part time job valeting cars at the local garage.

It kept him out from under Sylvia's feet and brought in some useful extra cash. When Sylvia died he was astonished to find that things no longer 'happened' around him in the house.

"I had to tell him to change his pyjamas," says Jenny. "He'd never lifted a finger for himself and had no idea about things like changing the sheets on the bed or shopping for food. Even when I pointed out all these things he took no notice. He was in denial.

"Dad expected me to replace my mother and to be there whenever he needed me. He had no conception of the pressure he was putting me under. He was completely insensitive. I talked it over with my sister and she said you can only do so much for someone when they are so selfish. He'd always been selfish."

Sylvia had been, in Jenny's words, "an absolutely wonderful wife who'd done everything in the house". "She smoothed the path for Dad so he never had to be involved in domestic chores of any kind. To be honest, I don't think Dad had a clue how hard Mum worked. He just took it all for granted. She looked after him as though he was a king, keeping him fit and strong and in very good health, so after she died Dad assumed I'd do the same."

Jenny's husband and teenage sons found it difficult to cope with the demands he was placing on their family life. Far from venerating the old man and revelling in his tales of life on the railways, they grew to resent his irritating ways and helpless dependence.

Sacrifices were many, especially when Jack's demands conflict-
ed with the family's needs. There were many times when Jenny
would have to tell the boys they couldn't do something, like
take part in a school play or, in her older son's case, start after-
school guitar lessons, because she couldn't guarantee there
would always be someone free to bring them home.

Neil, Jenny's youngest son, was due to take part in a Tae-Kwon-
Do competition one evening when Jack announced he had a
doctor's appointment and he expected Jenny to take him. "He
had me over a barrel," she says. "There was no-one else to take
him and he couldn't get there on his own, so I had no choice
but to get a friend to drop poor Neil off at the sports hall. I
managed to get along there later, but I'd missed seeing Neil
competing and being presented with a medal. I feel bad about
it to this day and I know Neil was upset."

That was just one incident in a long sequence that took a toll
on Jenny. The demands of her job, her busy role in the family
home and being on constant call for Jack meant she suffered
frequently from nervous exhaustion. She slept badly, too,
because she was always on edge, half expecting, always dread-
ing, the phone call, bringing her news that Jack had had another fall and needed her immediately. "I dreaded the phone
going because it usually meant there was some emergency. In
the sheltered flat he had a day warden and an alarm system, so
it was usually at night that I got the calls."

The falls resulted in Jack becoming increasingly disabled. He broke his leg twice and had to get around on an electric scooter. All through that torrid period of about three years, Jenny would go to Jack's GP to seek help for him with his drink problem, but, she says, "the doctor always treated it as a joke and never took me seriously".

"Whoever I saw would just laugh it off and say: 'My word, he's a character your Dad. He certainly likes his drop of whisky, doesn't he?' If it had been someone younger who was hospitalised through drink, they would have treated it and given help, but because it was an older person they thought it was amusing. They just couldn't see that I was crying out for help.

"I laugh when I see these things about caring for carers. As far as I have ever found, there is no care for carers. There's been nobody to help me, nobody to turn to."

The Princess Royal Trust for Carers (Helpline 020 7480 7788 **www. carers.org**) is the ideal organisation to help Ofcaps like Jenny. Unfortunately, she knew nothing of the charity's existence because the nearest branch to where she lives is 60 miles away. A carer support worker with PRTC says: "We can advocate for someone in Jenny's position. We would have put a lot of pressure on social services on her behalf. We would go to the GP with her, too. It doesn't matter what her father's like, it's the carer who is our concern.

"I sympathise with Jenny enormously. The trouble is, the statutory authorities are not good with alcoholism, nor are the homes. Sometimes it is necessary for someone in Jenny's position just to refuse to do any more. There will always be somewhere for somebody to be placed – but then the carer has to live with the guilt of that.

"The irony is that if Jenny had stopped caring for Jack he would have been helped, because social services have a statutory obligation. They can't just leave somebody in a dire situation.

"Sometimes people just need to be given permission to stop caring, so they don't feel bad about what they're doing. It's the poor person doing the propping up who keeps the situation stable so social services are not going to go in and spend money on it. They'll spend money on the person who hasn't got anybody to care for them."

Jenny says she felt Jack's mind was going when he was in hospital. She pinned a lot of hope on a diagnosis that would cause him to be moved into care. "I was in touch with social services all the time," she says, "and I'd be begging them to say to me 'he needs to be in a home'. But because he was so good at masking his problems they would assure me he was fine. They would give him a mental assessment test which he always passed, and that was the only yardstick they used. He was going through the motions for them. That was annoying. I got nowhere with that.

"My husband often lost patience because of Dad's demands and because of the way he would expect me to be at his beck and call. I felt torn all the time. I did what I felt was my duty for my mother's sake. I did what I know she would have wanted me to do. I guess my father and I didn't have the usual sort of relationship. I really didn't know if I loved him."

Various tests are used to indicate a patient's cognitive ability. The most commonly used one is the Mini Mental State Examination (MMSE) and it requires answers to a set of basic questions, such as naming colours and objects, recalling dates and giving personal information. Assessments involve mental health experts, who could be liaison nurses with mental health expertise, or consultants.

Should it be necessary, following the MMSE, a case conference follows, with patient and carers and the relevant health officials.

Decisions about the future care of a patient are made usually after several weeks during which the staff have got to know them and their home situation and after due consultation with all the people who need and are entitled to an input.

Joan's story

Joan's problems had started with a fall when she was 87. Already suffering with osteoporosis and Paget's Disease, a metabolic bone disorder which can cause muscle weakness and pain, the fall was the catalyst that ultimately took away her quality of life. The doctor at her cottage hospital was convinced no bones had been broken when she fell, and so it wasn't until Joan had endured three weeks of terrible pain that her daughter, Helen, managed to get her to a private consultant for a second opinion. This brought confirmation that she had, in fact, broken her hip.

Helen says she was extremely angry with the doctor who had made the original diagnosis, but he did at least apologise some months later. "Doctors are human," she says, "and there's nothing to be gained by harbouring grudges."

While still in hospital after the operation to pin the hip, Joan contracted MRSA. She was taken back to the operating theatre no fewer than five times for the wound to be cleaned. After such a painful and upsetting ordeal that lasted ten weeks, Joan was glad to be taken to a rehabilitation clinic, which Helen booked her into for a month.

This was where the characteristics of a cantankerous old woman first emerged, to Helen's horror. "The first time I visited Mum there, the nurses told me she'd been quite good in the night. They said she'd only rung the bell for attention 20 times. With a sinking heart, I realised that she'd already earned herself a reputation."

Joan learnt to walk a little with a frame but her confidence had gone and she was very miserable by the time Helen settled her back in her bungalow in Wales. Three months had passed since she'd last been at home and life was now very different. Most daily tasks that Joan had been able to do before, albeit slowly, were now beyond her and she became anxious and frustrated by her increasing immobility and inability to care for herself.

Having been proudly independent in running her own life up to the age of 86, it made it all the worse for Joan to have to ask for help with the smallest task and she took out her feelings of despair on everyone around her.

As neighbours, friends, carers and family rallied to help her in her distress, Joan treated all comers with contempt – shouting, ranting and abusing, so that by the end only the carers and Helen were left to bear the brunt of her resentment and fury. Everyone else had bowed out, their tolerance too strained and their feelings too hurt by the demanding harridan that Joan had become.

She was wilful. When she wanted to be a dear old lady she could be, Helen remembers, but she took advantage of people's kindness. "Being old gave her the freedom to abandon all normal niceties and human interaction," says Helen. "She no longer had any patience and was intolerant of others. Everything had to be done immediately and in the way that she wanted. She'd always been a bit of a control freak, but now she felt her age and situation meant she could manipulate and control everyone. She was like a spoilt toddler. Everything had to revolve around her completely.

"What I found so difficult to deal with was that here was my Mother, the person I'd always respected, but who had actually now become the child in our relationship. But, unlike with a two year old, I couldn't use parental discipline. I found her impossible to deal with."

Helen employed almost military-like strategies in devising and overseeing a daily rota of care for Joan. Although her work kept her in London, she was closely involved in all aspects of her Mother's life and was constantly referred to for decisions. Her brother, who lived a five hour drive away from his Mother, visited regularly but found the verbal abuse so alienating and upsetting that he usually told her that he couldn't stand it and would turn round and head back home again, preferring the long drive to any more time spent in Joan's company.

"My brother was not prepared to put up with what I put up with and, in a way, one cannot blame him," Helen says. "My daughter, too, used to get very angry because she couldn't bear to hear Grandma speaking to me in the way she did. Because Mum didn't like to see her granddaughter cross, she never wanted her to come down with me, so they didn't see much of each other in the final years. That saddened me.

"There were a few occasions when my daughter came with me and my brother came as well. Mum hated that because we would talk with each other and she would feel excluded. She'd become completely hysterical – anything to regain our full attention."

Ofcaps inevitably get to know their parent better in a caring situation than they ever have done before. With the closeness and intimacy comes the discovery of traits that you may never have known existed, which can be both a privilege and a disappointment. It's when those traits include downright bad behaviour that it's something of a shock.

The problem can be started by Mum or Dad having quite unrealistic expectations, turning them into a demanding old so-and-so. Mum may think 'I looked after my Mother, so why can't my daughter look after me in the way I want?' They can't get their heads round the fact many daughters work nowadays so they can't be there at their beck and call.

You see them in a new light, but it's when they see you in a dim light that the sparks can fly.

Bill's story

The pleasure of having gentle, even-tempered Bill under the same roof was felt by all the family when Beverley, Alec and daughter Becky welcomed him into their house. But what they had all seen as the solution to Bill's lonely widower's existence in his bungalow a short distance away across town wasn't quite as perfect as they'd imagined.

"It was a gradual thing," says Beverley. "Basically, Dad just never seemed to need or to want privacy. It dawned on us after a while that he was always, but always, there, wherever we were in the house. And this was how it was going to be for a long, long time. This was the reality of what I'd hoped would be nice but which very definitely wasn't."

Beverley readily admits to being ashamed by her feelings. "How can I complain about my circumstances which seem trivial compared with a lot of people?" she says. "But while the seriousness of our situation may not compare, I still have the responsibility. And because I've still got family at home I have divided loyalties. Let's face it, when you've got toothache and someone next to you has had a leg off, it doesn't mean to say that your toothache hurts you any less."

It was nothing enormous or catastrophic, just numerous little things that Bill did that built up and up into furious heads of steam in Beverley, Alec and Becky. Basically, as they all know, he is a kind and loving man with a sweet and generous nature. But he is also stubborn, deeply set in his ways, unsociable and insensitive, characteristics which make for a fraught atmosphere in a shared home. And when that home contains an already well-established family unit, where husband and wife both work long days in demanding jobs and where a young schoolgirl is becoming a teenager packed full of explosive hormones, the coexistence is immediately lacking a certain gentle harmony.

The television was a major bone of contention. Bill's choice of viewing was very different from the family's and, because they were out of the house during the day, he would take up residence in the sitting-room and retain charge of the remote control even once they'd got home. The notion of fitting in with them and considering their wishes either did not appeal or did not cross his mind.

"I often used to think it was because he was a man that he seemed so insensitive," says Beverley. "Maybe a woman would be more intuitive and responsive to situations."

She had thought Bill would start going out a bit more once he had moved. He had no outside interests or hobbies that occupied him in the home, so Beverley tried to encourage him to join activities and go to day centres where he would meet others of his age.

But the opposite happened. Because he no longer needed to make the effort to go out shopping and care for his own home, his life revolved entirely around the house and his hobby became watching television soaps and game shows.

The very fact that Bill was always there, and never in his room watching his own TV, jangled everyone's nerves and frayed their tempers, especially when Beverley and Alec returned from work and needed, or simply just wanted, to talk together.

Like a lot of elderly people, Bill's hearing is not good but he refuses to wear a hearing aid. He has selective hearing, Beverley says, so that he doesn't hear what he's meant to hear, even though he pretends he has heard and understood, but he can pick up a whispered confidence at 50 metres. Having to retreat to the garden for a private chat, or wait until Bill had gone to bed, added to the family's growing resentment.

Many elderly people have hearing difficulties. Some ignore them and battle on in a world that seems to have become mysteriously quieter with the passing years. Popular survival tactics among the hard of hearing are:

1   Turning the television up to a level which threatens a tidal wave in the goldfish bowl

2   Judiciously turning the head and cupping the 'good' ear to catch the occasional word in a conversation

3   The ludicrous, but extremely common, gently nodding head to indicate that everything has been heard (not) and understood (not)

4   The slightly distracted faraway look, as if to indicate that listening is for wimps

Other older people, recognising that their personal audio equipment isn't as pin sharp as it once was, willingly go for hearing tests.

However, it is acknowledged that hearing aids are not always the solution because too many of them are outdated and inefficient. The Royal National Institute for the Deaf says that audiology services, already under great pressure, are in need of modernisation and improvement, as is the provision of hearing aids.

Ofcaps need to be aware that hearing impairment can reduce the quality of Mum or Dad's life and could lead to depression and social isolation. You should also be warned of the well-known phenomenon that someone who cannot hear when they're being asked if they've taken their tablets or been to the loo, can hear every syllable of a private conversation the other side of a closed door.

Consider fixing Mum or Dad up with a set of headphones if they insist on watching TV with the sound turned up enough to annoy the neighbours. They could pass for cool among their grandchildren who think only DJs wear headphones, but it does make sense if it prevents complaints from anyone likely to be disturbed by *The Learning Zone* at 4.30am.

The bathroom became the focus of regular skirmishes in Beverley's house. While she and Alec had their own en suite, Becky shared the family bathroom with Bill, a creature of habit not easily deflected from any long-established routine. This meant that if he had always gone into the bathroom at 8.03am, then that's what he still expected to do. Finding Becky locked in there at that time as she prepared for her school day meant a lot of unholy shouting and banging, with Bill demanding access and complaining that Becky was inconsiderate.

The situation could only be resolved by keeping the bathroom warriors apart, so Alec, a builder, put in an en suite for Bill in the corner of his bedroom. But Grandpa's relationship with his once adoring Becky was severely damaged, and she had little to do with him after that wedge had been driven between them. Friends' houses held more appeal as an after-school destination and she spent more and more time away from home.

One of the pleasures of being part of a united family is seeing the mutual benefits of the relationship between grandchild and grandparents where love and happiness tend to be unconditional. This creates an intense closeness that in some circumstances can eclipse even the parent-child bond.

The dynamics are radically altered when Grandma or Grandpa becomes a dependant. Now the child sees their grandparent in a very different light and in situations that need explaining with tact and kindness. Don't exclude grandchildren from knowledge that will help them understand what's going on and that could explain why, for example, Grandma now sounds different, doesn't recognise them, can't walk very well or gets very irritable.

The age gap between the two generations has more of an impact as time goes on. By the time the grandchild is a teenager the relationship with their grandparent may be threatened by exasperation. If the parents 'don't understand' then Grandma or Grandpa almost certainly doesn't. But a grandchild in their teens can play a valuable role in helping with Grandma's care and comfort and, as lessons in life go, this one is no less important than learning how to stay solvent.

Alec, too, was increasingly finding excuses either not to go straight home after work or to disappear as soon as he came in. He couldn't face seeing his father-in-law, hunched in the sitting room, TV remote in hand, seeing yet not seeing, hearing yet not hearing, every minute aspect of the family's life – and then passing comment on it. While Becky was constantly quizzed by Bill on where she was going, what time she'd got in last night, whether she'd be warm enough going out without a cardigan, who she was seeing, so too was Alec questioned interminably about the current building project.

One of the changes made when Bill moved in was to give him the bedroom which Alec had used as a study. Alec built a replacement office in the garden, and that's where he would often escape to in the evenings. "I felt I was losing Alec," says Beverley. "I'm not exaggerating when I say it got to the stage where our marriage was really in jeopardy. We finally had to confront our problems when my elder daughter said that Alec was going to her house after work to avoid coming home and would we please do something about it. I felt so guilty. So of course we had to talk. We couldn't see an immediate solution but we knew something had to be done."

Most Ofcaps experience large doses of guilt at various stages. It doesn't take hours on a psychiatrist's couch to seek out the reason, either. It's because, quite simply, you're dealing with a parent, the person who taught us our responsibilities in the first place and to whom we are unendingly indebted. The greater the love bestowed, the greater the debt and, invariably, the greater the feelings of guilt.

Guilt is a concomitant of caring – those who care the most have the greatest feelings of guilt. Nine times out of 10, Ofcaps are not justified in feeling guilty but they almost have to absolve themselves. If the guilt is not helped it can spill over into anger, which can lead to lashing out and then the guilt comes back a hundredfold.

Try taking a step back and examining whether your emotions have been influenced by love for your parent or by guilt. The answer is probably both, in which case do stop beating yourself up and remember that guilt is destructive, negative and pointless. As an Ofcap you can't afford to expend emotional effort on something so wasteful. Put guilt where it belongs – in the minds of those whose antisocial behaviour demonstrates a woeful lack of conscience.

May's story

Douglas's Extraction of Mother from the old family home to a purpose-built development for over 70s went mercifully smoothly. May, ever the trouper, rose to the occasion and seemed never even to look back, in any sense, once her daughter-in-law Carol drove her away to start a new life in Surrey. With her two grown-up granddaughters helping as well as Douglas and Carol, May's settling in process was more light-hearted fun than soul-searching regret.

Much hard work had gone on in advance, so that there were curtains up and carpets laid throughout the new flat before May arrived. She'd only seen pictures of the apartment block, but she was confident all would be well. "I'm ready to move," she'd announced to Douglas in the early stages of the Extraction plan. "It'll make life easier for me and I know it will be good for you because you won't have to keep driving all the way over here to see me and worrying about me when you're not here." All the family agreed that her positive attitude made the whole task simpler and more bearable.

Douglas says May needed frequent lectures about handling unwanted phone calls. Despite being told, repeatedly, simply to hang up on them, she found it difficult not to engage the caller in polite conversation. "Don't do it, Mother, we'd tell her," says Douglas. "They're not being nice to you when they chat, they're trying to get money out of you. Fortunately, the calls reduced once we registered her number with the Telephone Preference Service." (Helpline 0845 070 0707 **www.tpsonline.org.uk**)

May settled contentedly into her first-floor flat, immediately appreciating the security it afforded and enjoying the views which, though different from the pastoral scenes around her old home, were of trees, public gardens and a river, so that she could watch the changing seasons. The complex offered sheltered living in one- and two-bedroom flats with communal facilities such as a dining room, a lounge and a hobbies room. Lifts and wide doorways meant any flat was suitable for wheelchair users, and there was non-medical help available night and day either by pre-arrangement or, in an emergency, by pulling a cord fitted within easy reach in every room.

For anyone incapacitated it offered a comfortable way of life. For a fully fit 88 year old like May it was luxury indeed, especially after her somewhat Spartan way of life in rural Norfolk. However, it came at a considerable price. First of all the flat itself – and May chose a two-bed one so that she would have as much space as possible for all her belongings – was bought for a sum that would probably have secured a three-bedroom family home in the same town, and then there were the monthly charges payable to the management company.

"Places like this are not for church mice," says Douglas. "They're actually very expensive, though I hesitate to say extortionately so because how do you put a price on the peace of mind they can give old people and the feeling of being settled in safe and congenial surroundings? Mother was fortunate to have sold a biggish house and to have had some savings to finance the purchase of the flat and her outgoings, but there wasn't a bottomless pit by any means. The money wouldn't last for ever, so she needed to be aware of that."

Fortunately, May had a make-do-and-mend attitude to most things in life and her needs were modest. She restricted her weekly outgoings to no more than the sum she received in state pension, enabling income from investments to pay the larger bills.

Only a very small proportion of elderly people enjoy the sort of comfort and relative affluence of someone in May's situation. Most have to struggle to get by, with the constant worry that soon they may not be able to make ends meet. Their worries in turn become their Ofcaps' worries, and the prospect of long term illness or disablement adds to the very real fears for the future.

There are benefits and allowances available to people who fall into various categories, but few would consider them adequate. Fewer still would think they were generous, and virtually no-one would agree they are easy to obtain or simple to understand. This is where an Ofcap can flex muscles and ensure Mum or Dad's rights are upheld. It's easy to admit defeat when faced with so much bureaucracy, but be tenacious and, as in all cases when you're not sure of your ground, get help from experts. The Citizens Advice Bureau (**www.adviceguide.org.uk**) or Age Concern are good starting points.

May found life most agreeable in her new surroundings. She made friends among her immediate neighbours and enjoyed walking into town along a riverside path. She insisted she didn't miss her garden and was happy to walk around the council tended park and admire its borders without feeling compelled to get on her knees to do the weeding.

Either Douglas or Carol, sometimes both, would call and spend time with May four or five times a week, and they would sometimes scoop her up and take her to their house to share lunch or to meet their friends over supper. She had made it clear to them when she moved that she didn't want them to feel obliged to include her in their lives, so when they did have her over for social occasions it was always through choice and not duty.

Younger son Hugh, still living near Nice on the French Riviera, appeared on May's doorstep about twice a year, usually on his way to visit friends in Devon. He rang her every couple of months for a chat and kept in touch with Douglas by phone and email, but was only peripherally involved in his mother's life.

Tension between siblings can arise, as we know, at any point twixt cradle and grave, and sometimes it is there all the time. When it exists between Ofcaps it's particularly unfortunate because unity is strength when dealing with family matters.

The division of duties, chores and responsibilities is almost invariably uneven, with the greater burden falling on whichever Ofcap lives nearer, or is older, or has a less demanding job, or is more capable, more bossy, more savvy. Any sibling or siblings in a less involved role will then run the risk of being thought of as less caring and less loving, even though they themselves may feel marginalised and impotent. You can't win. Such situations are almost bound to breed resentment on both sides, unless you are lucky enough to have an exceptionally good relationship.

Conversely, the Ofcap who does the most for Mum is often seen as the one with the greatest warts because they're always there, always dealing with the tricky issues, having to nag a bit, perhaps, and even having to make unpopular decisions. Therefore the absent, less proactive Ofcap can become idolised. Cue several extra tons of resentment.

Not many Ofcap siblings get through without the occasional sharp words or a firm put-down. Most of those interviewed for this book had something critical to say about a family member, usually a sibling, for not pulling their weight or for showing lack of gumption or sensitivity. "It's not interference that I need from my sister," says one, "but the feeling that we are both party to some of the difficult decisions, and that there is someone to share the responsibility. And someone else to do some visiting would break it up a bit."

Bear in mind that inter-sibling warfare is deeply upsetting for a parent to witness, so if you've got a spat going on, do it in private. And get it over with. Ofcaps didn't get where they are today by wasting energy on battles in their own backyard, so do count to 10 and try and keep the peace.

Six years of happy equilibrium followed May's move to her new flat, but two months after her 94th birthday she suffered a stroke. Carol was with her at the time, otherwise the outcome might have been horribly different.

An ambulance took May to hospital, where, after numerous tests and a scan, it was found that she had indeed suffered a stroke – something which, by this time, most people suspected. For this frail old lady, and for her family, life was going to be very different from now on.

Although a stroke can occur at any age, more than three-quarters (98,000) are in people over the age of 65. It is the third largest cause of death after heart disease and cancer and the greatest cause of disability in the UK, with about a quarter of a million people affected at any one time. About 70,000 people in the UK die from stroke each year.

There are two types of stroke. The vast majority, 80%, are caused by blood clots in the brain, while 20% occur when blood vessels burst. In both cases, the brain is starved of oxygen, damaging or killing cells.

Treatment through drugs is the norm after a stroke and, as sufferers are often left with difficulty walking, talking and performing other basic tasks, rehabilitation through physiotherapy and occupational therapy is often used to improve speech and movement.

Norah's story

Only two years after she'd become a widow herself, Sally had been diagnosed with breast cancer. Her treatment involved a lumpectomy and radiotherapy and frequent follow-up checks. It was a bleak period, especially as she hardly had her life back on track after 18 months of nursing her husband through motor neurone disease. She was 38 when he died, but she says she felt more like 98.

"Being told I had cancer was the most shattering blow possible after what the girls and I had been through," she says. Norah was very supportive through the tragedy of Alex's death and Sally's own illness. But that was when Ted was still around. With Ted gone, Norah's emotions lost their prop and, alongside her lack of self-confidence, she had occasional panic attacks and would only leave her house to go to Sally's next door or to the convenience store just round the corner where all the staff knew her.

"By this time Mum had been widowed for about two and a half years," says Sally. "I had hoped that she would be pulling through a bit better, but if anything she seemed to be getting worse. She was under the weather all the time and I was quite concerned about her. The nit-picking and nagging over the girls continued, along with the clucking disapproval over my work commitments, but she wasn't coming to our house as often as she had been so the carping became slightly more bearable."

Even having a dog to care for didn't encourage Norah to get out of the house much. Despite lavishing an inordinate amount of love and affection on Brad, her Yorkshire terrier, she never felt inclined to give it any exercise beyond the confines of the garden.

Norah's reluctance to leave home meant that she'd left it far too late for treatment when she finally confided in Sally that she, too, had a lump in her breast. "She admitted she'd had it for ages," says Sally, "and she was utterly terrified. By the time she showed me and I managed to get her to see her GP, her whole breast had turned black. It was terrible."

Sally suspects that it wasn't just her Mother's fragile emotional state that played its part in keeping Norah at home, but a desire for privacy in personal matters that is typical of her generation. "If she'd had a problem with her hand or a foot it would have been different, I'm sure," she says, "but Mum is like a lot of women of her age who are uncomfortable talking about things like breasts and bodily functions. She was embarrassed but also very frightened, so we had a lot of talking to do and a lot of decisions to make about the future."

One in three people will get cancer at some time in their lives, which is a jolly thought. However, two in three won't get it, which is a better statistic to dwell upon. And survival rates are improving all the time, thanks to breakthroughs in research and advances in treatment.

There are 200 different types of cancer and age is known to be the greatest risk factor. Add 'stage' to age, and you get a more reliable prognosis: if a cancer is detected and treated at an earlier stage, the chance of survival is greater. One that is left to an advanced stage puts life at severe risk.

CHAPTER 4

Declaration of dependence

At this stage, like it or not, their life is in your hands – and, guess what, your life is in their hands. Nothing will ever be the same again. You will soon learn not to think about planning a holiday or wondering who to have round at Christmas. Your life is not your life any more – it has changed shape dramatically to accommodate a life that can barely exist without you, one that has aspects to it that will sometimes amaze and often appal.

Facing the uncertainty of the future with your Mum or Dad so dependent on you is both a blessing and a burden. Some Ofcaps say they see it as a privilege, others regard the inconvenience and upheaval as an untenable imposition.

Whichever way you look at it, you have in your hands the fragile life of someone who is depending on you to be their link with the world and to keep the more unpleasant aspects of it at bay.

Whether this is played out in their own home, in your home, in a nursing or residential home, a hospice or a hospital, have no doubt that it is to you that your parent looks for strength and reassurance. By virtue of their age alone, they know the end is, if not nigh, then certainly nigh on nigh, but when a debilitating illness or disability is added to the equation, then they'll inevitably sense a lowering of the curtains.

All their lives, your Mum or Dad will have held the medical profession in awe. Their doctor can do no wrong and every utterance is obeyed and repeated, as though it were from the Book of Common Prayer. 'My doctor' is up there in the pantheon of greats, alongside the Queen Mother, Sir Winston Churchill and that nice Mr Dimbleby. Now, finding themselves dropped into a world of consultants, specialists, nurses-with-strange-titles, trolleys, porters, lifts, drips, bedpans and grapes, they don't know who to turn to or to trust any more – except you.

Anyone over the age of 50 expecting a hospital to be the same sort of place it was when they had their tonsils out at the age of 11 is in for a shock, so an Ofcap with a parent in this position needs to prepare them for the experience. Cynics might suggest mugging up on how to maintain self-esteem while lying on a trolley in a corridor, or an evening class in map reading (some hospitals can be enormous, with confusing signage), and, perhaps top of the list, a degree in anger management so that they know how to sit and wait for hours on end without exploding with frustration and fury.

'I'll take you to your hospital appointment, Mum,' you say cheerfully, anticipating a there-and-back-in-an-hour type of expedition. Best write off at least half a day – and don't forget a pocket of change for the hospital car park, for when Mum forgets to bring the pass that she might have been sent.

Fortunately, more people have a good experience in hospital than a bad one, but it's the bad ones we tend to hear about and they're what fuel our prejudices. You can help allay Mum or Dad's fears by preparing for the best, not the worst. Generally, hospital staff are constructive and sympathetic and they want to be helpful. If you encounter an obstructive one, go to the next level up. (See Chapter Five for more on this topic.)

Be aware that since 1991 patients have had the statutory right to see their medical records but this is not always as easy as it should be. The Patients' Association (020 8423 9111 **www.patients-association.com**) has a guide to obtaining access to records, including *pro forma* letters you can use and what to do if you experience difficulties. An Ofcap trying to get a parent's medical records is unlikely to make much progress because of the Data Protection Act. (Data protection helpline 01625 545 745)

Joan's story

For the last three years of her life, feisty Joan was looked after in her home. NHS carers came in three times a day for a total of six hours while the other 18 hours were covered by private carers, paid for by daughter Helen. Unfortunately, Joan made life so difficult for her carers that they could not tolerate being with her for more than two hours at a time. This meant that, as the carers came from the nearest town 20 minutes' drive away, Helen was also having to pay 40 minutes' travel time for each of them.

Many people played their part in ensuring Helen kept her promise to Joan that she would remain at home for as long as possible. Everybody came to the house, including the chiropodist, physiotherapist and the entire team of carers. Helen says her mother was very grateful and was totally aware of all that was going on. "She would say, all the time, when she wasn't shouting at one of us, that she realised she would not be there if it were not for what I was doing."

Joan was also aware of the expense involved in keeping her at home and often expressed her concern. Helen reassured her, saying there was no cause to fret. "But I was secretly worrying about where I would get the money from if she lived for very much longer," she says. "My brother and I discussed various ways of solving the problem if she lived to be 100. We looked at creating a self-contained flat in the garage of her bungalow so that she could have a live-in carer, which I thought would probably be the ultimate solution."

Wales social services were magnificent, Helen says. "They were utterly wonderful. They provided carers to get her up in the morning, to prepare her lunch and her tea, and to put her to bed. They were lovely – the kindest, most smashing women you could hope to meet.

"It was social services, too, that organised special loo hoists, a thing to raise her chair, to raise her bed, a special mattress so she wouldn't get bed sores, all sorts of things to help her. It was amazing – they were a fabulous team of ladies. Only one of them couldn't cope with my mother, who managed to offend her so much that she never came back."

There is an astonishing range of items, from two handled teacups to walk-in baths, designed to make living easier for disabled people, the wheel-chair user, the bed bound, those recovering from operations or any older person who finds too many obstacles in daily life.

Take your pick from such goodies as:

- Shock absorbing crutches
- A mattress elevator
- A slatted bath seat
- A zipped bag in which to carry a raised toilet seat
- A puller-upper for tights and stockings

Then there's an array of ingenious gadgets to help arthritic hands remove plugs, turn keys, switch on lights and operate taps.

In short, there is something for just about every eventuality, but whether Mum or Dad's social services will come up trumps with what they need depends on a number of factors – availability, funding and the efficiency of the organisation. Yes, you have it in one: it's a lottery.

While many high streets have a specialist shop that stocks hundreds of items for disabled people, it can be profitable to think laterally. My Mum bought a beautifully simple stick-seat from a fishing tackle shop at a fraction of the price of a 'disabled' one. For advice and guidance, contact the Disabled Living Foundation on 0845 130 9177 **www.dlf.org.uk**.

Joan's total emotional dependence on Helen even extended as far as needing to know where she was at all times. If Helen was not at work or at her home in London, perhaps out for an evening or away for a weekend, Joan had to have the address and phone number and the name of whoever she was with. "This was terribly wearing," Helen says. "It was as though I had a dependent child to cope with. She had to be able to contact me at all times. If she didn't know where I was she would panic."

One weekend Helen took her daughter on a long-promised visit to Cambridge. Joan was furious when she learnt where they were, even though she was assured that the weather was awful enough to be spoiling it for them and was also making the prospect of the drive home rather worrying. "You should have come to see me," Joan shouted down the phone. "And then if you'd been killed on the road it would have been worthwhile."

The only way Helen coped when she took over the 24-hour caring role on alternate weekends was to accept that she would never be able to do enough and would never be able to do anything right. "That was quite a significant breakthrough," she recalls. "Up to that point I'd tried to be perfect and do whatever she wanted at her beck and call, but once I'd accepted that this was simply not possible, the situation became easier to live with.

"I also reminded myself that I still had other roles to fulfil, like being in a full time job and being a mother and I was not being cruel or unkind if I couldn't do absolutely everything she wanted me to do. I learnt not to beat myself up over things that were just not achievable.

"They were long, long days. For 14 hours a day she wasn't content unless I was within one foot of her. I couldn't even go to the loo without her shouting at me to come back. She was only happy if I was sitting there with her. I didn't even have to be speaking. I just had to be there. Right by her.

"I'd sometimes have to say 'Look Mum – I've got to go out. I've got to get something'. 'Oh don't leave me,' she'd wail. 'You can't leave me alone like this.' And then there'd be tears. She could wind me up like nobody's business. The only way I could manage was to detach myself. I would go into the kitchen and if she called me I simply didn't go in to her. I'd tell her I was going to make her lunch and wouldn't be coming back in for a quarter of an hour. If she wanted to spend a penny, of course I'd go to her, but I had to try and ignore all her false alarms, which was terribly difficult."

At night it was not a shout or a cry that alerted Helen, but a bell or, as she remembers it, "that bloody bell!" "Two o'clock in the morning she'd ring the bell and keep ringing it until I appeared. 'I'm uncomfortable,' she'd say, or 'Can you just move this a little bit?' and it would be something that she wanted moved an inch. Then she'd ring for me again at three o'clock. This time she didn't want anything, just for me to sit with her, not speaking, just to be with her. That bell would go and if it wasn't answered immediately she would go doolally."

Responding to a cry for help is instinctive – just think how we react when we hear a baby or child in distress. The same instinct is in Ofcaps, ever alert to the call from an incapacitated Mum or Dad. The trouble is, the calls can be so frequent that they get ingrained in the consciousness, like the familiar chimes of a clock, so that they go unheard.

Replacing the calls with a bell is a good idea, if only the hand in charge of the bell can be encouraged to ring only when it is really necessary, especially at night. It's not easy to impose such a reasonable discipline, as Helen can vouch, but as a general means of summoning help, a bell has it over the thump of a stick on the bedroom floor.

Trust the Ofcap to respond and to be there. But can you always trust the paid care worker in his or her absence? Apparently not, according to one former care agency worker, who says she had a number of colleagues who considered it a matter of pride to put in the least amount of work they could get away with. A half-hour visit by one of them to a lonely old man would in reality amount to a few minutes to empty his commode. A quick in and out, when what the man, and thousands like him, really want is someone to sit and chat.

Ofcaps beware: check what's happening – or not happening – in your absence. For peace of mind, turn to a wonderful service like Crossroads (01788 573653 **www.crossroads.org.uk**), which provides trained carers to look after the person in the usual carer's absence. For Ofcaps this could make the difference between coping and going under.

Bill's story

The drip, drip, drip of Bill's interrogation, which always managed to irritate because of its nature and timing, got through to Beverley too, so that she found herself climbing up walls with suppressed fury. "If he asked me once in the course of a day if the dishwasher was full he must have asked me a hundred times," she says. "There were so many silly, trivial little things that obviously obsessed him, because his world was terribly small, but he couldn't see that they weren't important to us."

Bill's permanent presence in front of the family's TV set became a problem that needed to be tackled, especially as the solution was obvious. Beverley gently persuaded him to go upstairs to his room and take his nightly 'fix' of soaps on his own TV.

That small triumph of persuading Bill to change his evening routine gave Beverley the courage to suggest one or two other areas where adjustments could be made to restore some harmony. But Bill resisted, with much grumbling and complaining. "It was quite a clever manipulation on his part because each time I said to him, just gently, 'Oh Dad, do you think you could do this?' or 'Could you not do that?' he would say: 'I knew I was going to be a burden. I knew I shouldn't have come here.' It was dreadfully upsetting. It got to the stage where I didn't ask him to do anything because I was afraid of getting this reaction.

"It makes me sound horrible and heartless, but it is the way he played it out. I don't know if it was a conscious thing on his part, or subconscious, but I played right into it by not wanting to upset him and then bottling things up rather than confronting situations."

The head-of-steam syndrome can crop up in all sorts of circumstances. You don't have to be under the same roof as Mum or Dad or even within 100 miles, for something they say to set light to your blue touchpaper. Just imagine all those teeth being gritted and all those telephones being held away from the ear while Ofcaps all over the country try to avoid self-detonation.

Avoid these unhappy situations by adopting a code word for use when a topic is off limits or taboo or if you are just too exhausted or distracted to enter into a discussion. If, say, Mum or Dad brings up the subject of your children's lifestyles, you can, by mutual pre-arrangement, invoke the code word and shelve the matter. Work it out between you and you could have fun. There's a certain devilment to be enjoyed in one of you saying 'portcullis' (a more polite version of 'shut up') and ending potentially damaging talk.

Beverly admits to making a huge mistake in not dealing early on with the festering anger and resentment. She knows she should have given Bill an opportunity at the beginning to say what he did or didn't like. "I felt for him," she says, "because he obviously felt that he couldn't say what he'd like to say because he was in our house. Giving up his own house had been a huge thing for him."

Bill paid £60 a week towards his costs. Beverley says she never itemised the bills but imagines that the main expenditure was on heating. Because he was sitting in the house all day, he had the central heating on and, quite often, the gas fire as well. "We bought him a lovely blanket to put over his knees but he never used it," says Beverley. Bill's use of the heating caused tensions, especially with Alec, and they all felt uncomfortable when they came home on a spring day to find the house boiling hot because Bill was still sitting with the heating full on.

When Alec put in the en suite bathroom for him they contacted social services for financial help but instantly hit a series of brick walls so gave up. As Beverley says: "We didn't have the time to persevere. I was also told that it might be possible to get some sort of allowance, possibly an attendance allowance, because of Dad's mobility problems. A huge pack of information and forms came through the door, so off-putting and impenetrable that none of it ever got touched."

It is well known that the forms are daunting, even for the super intelligent and confident. Because of this, a number of organisations, such as the Citizens Advice Bureau and Age Concern, offer a form-filling service either at home or at the local office. The Benefits Agency (08457 123 456) will also help by filling in the form and posting it back for you to sign.

An Age Concern volunteer says: "It's surprising how many people give up too easily when there is help available. Making a successful application ensures that the person receives what they are entitled to, and that's only right. It is important to make it clear on the forms what Mum or Dad's very worst situation is. For example, if the form asks how many times they need help to get out of a chair, it may only be once a day but it will be every day, so they must say that they can't get out of a chair without help."

Basically, it's the help that's needed, not the help that's given, that determines an application.

Attendance Allowance is a non-means tested tax free benefit paid by the Department for Work and Pensions and decisions on new applications (from over 65s, sick or disabled) are made by the Disability Benefit Unit. It is paid to those with a physical disability or mental health needs and who have needed care or supervision for six months before applying. Those with a terminal illness qualify automatically.

'Care' means help with personal care, day-to-day personal tasks, getting dressed, turning over in bed, taking baths or showers. 'Supervision' means the need for someone watching out to prevent injury or harm.

There are two rates of Attendance Allowance:

1   The lower rate (currently £40.55 a week) is if care or supervision is needed either during the day or during the night

2   The higher rate (£60.60 a week) is if care or supervision is needed both during the day and the night

Fill in form AA1A from the Post Office or the Department of Work and Pensions or a claim can be registered on the benefits helpline on 0800 882 200. Return the completed claim pack within six weeks to ensure it is backdated.

For further guidance through this murky gloom, consult **www.disability. gov.uk** and **www.direct.gov.uk**. If an Ofcap plans to claim Carer's Allowance, then apply at the same time (Carer's Allowance Unit 01253 856123).

Although Alec and Beverley knew that Bill's generous nature meant he would always be willing to lend or give them money if they needed it, they also knew that they were going to need a lot more than a cash gift if they were to maintain their standard of living into retirement. To this end, they put together a plan that would, with hard work, ensure the raising of collateral by moving house at regular intervals over the next six years. They would start by downsizing to a two-bedroom cottage, with enough space for them and Becky, and then progress back up the ladder, using Alec's building skills to ensure a good profit from each sale.

The first move, to the small cottage that Alec was already doing up, would mean a new start for the family – but where would it leave Bill?

"Without the plan we would have just gone chugging along," says Beverley. "But we would have hit a problem in due course because Dad wasn't going to be able to go on using the stairs for an awful lot longer. There was always that spectre lurking of what on earth we would do when that day dawned.

"But the plan gave us an escape route. Not to put too fine a point on it, we had felt trapped. With the plan, we could see a way forward – but it came at a terrible price."

To start with, Beverley had to explain about the plan to Bill. Alec promised he'd be with her when she told him, but it was still, she admits, the most difficult thing she had ever done in her life.

"By this time we'd known for a while what we were going to do, to sell up and move, and that he would have to move somewhere else or come with us into a rented place temporarily. Dad's a terrible flapper, and frets and mulls things over, so I tend not to tell him things until the very last minute so as to cause the least upset.

"We had been told there was a vacancy at the local Abbeyfield but they wanted an early decision. Alec and I had been to have a look at it and were very impressed, so now I needed to explain everything to Dad and tell him the options.

"It was truly awful. We were rocking his world. It was heart-breaking to see the expression on his face. He didn't want to leave and said so quite clearly. He was horrified, and he was also worried about the financial implications."

Bill's reaction of total devastation was even worse than Beverley had feared. "I've been so happy here," he told her. "I thought I was here for the rest of my life. I don't want anything to change. How can you drag me away and put me somewhere I don't want to go?"

Beverley felt she had betrayed him and let him down, especially when he said: "If I'd known this was going to happen, I would never have come to live with you in the first place. I would never have left my bungalow because I was happy there." He didn't understand that the family might have moved house two or three years ago but they stayed put for his sake.

If the offer from Abbeyfield had not been made, then Beverley is certain she would not have persevered with the plan. "We did give him the option of not going but of staying with us," she says, "although it would have meant going into rented accommodation instead of the cottage until our next property was ready."

The decision was finally made when Beverley and Alec took Bill to look round Abbeyfield. He was very impressed – but continued to express his misgivings and unhappiness.

The Abbeyfield Society was founded in 1956 as a solution to problems of loneliness and isolation among older people through offering them homes where they could live together with care and companionship. Alongside a balance of privacy and caring support is a measure of independent living for those no longer happy to live alone or share with others.

There are 800 Abbeyfield homes around the UK, run by 500 member societies, providing accommodation for more than 8,000 residents and involving 10,000 volunteers. Each home has a resident house manager and acceptance into an Abbeyfield home is by interview to determine compatibility with the other residents. (Abbeyfield HQ: 01727 857536 **www.abbeyfield.com**)

When Bill was told that the vacancy was his, he was less than enthusiastic. Beverley assured him he didn't have to go there if he really didn't want to but he said, with considerable ill will, that he would go. The family were sure he would have a much better quality of life and he would be much safer. A fall at home while everyone was out was becoming more and more likely and, being a stubborn old man, he refused to wear an alarm around his neck.

"Although I know that he has felt cared for and loved, my guilt is so bad it hurts," says Beverley. "I've let him down, I know that.

"I have a confession to make that shows how much I've let

myself down, too. One morning I was in the kitchen when I realised that Dad hadn't come down from his room. It wasn't like him to be late – everything was always done on the dot. I wondered what the problem was. I was on the point of going up to check and then I was aware that I was thinking: *this could be a relief in a way.* I can't believe that I had such a horrible, horrible thought.

"Compared with some of my friends' parents, he's an absolute pussycat. He's never been awful or mean or interfered with the children's upbringing – it's just the pressures of sharing our home with somebody else. Sadly, I didn't feel he was my Dad when he was living with us – he was just a presence in the house.

"I regret I made the decision in the first place to offer him the opportunity to come and live with us. And he regrets it, too. But it was done with the best of intentions, as most cock-ups usually are."

The biggest three mistakes they made, says Beverley, was that there was no self-contained accommodation for Bill, that they failed to establish ground rules from the outset, and that they didn't open clear lines of communication.

You have to remember, she says, that when they're in your home they're not your parent any more. They become like your children but you can't tell them what you want them to do – yet they are dependent on you. You have the responsibility without any of the authority.

Beverley says she has been deeply saddened by the deterioration in the relationship between Bill and his granddaughter, Becky, but she is hopeful it can be rekindled. As for Alec, he became noticeably more at ease with Bill as soon as the plan was formalised and there are signs of their former close friendship being re-established.

She says it was when she heard Alec explaining their plan to friends that she knew it was all for the best. He flashed them a big smile and told them he was looking forward to getting his wife back. "Believe me, that made me cry."

Ofcaps' partners are in a very difficult position, stuck there in the seat beside their mate on the crazy roller-coaster ride. 'Tiptoeing over broken glass' is how one husband describes his experience, while another says he feels guilty about his resentment at being pushed down the pecking order when his mother-in-law's needs are being attended to.

Their most useful role is a supportive, consultative one with, where appropriate, occasional outbreaks of a practical nature for Mum or Dad in-law, whether it be cooking meals, doing the garden or repainting a couple of window frames. However, Ofcaps should be conscious of their partner's limits of tolerance. It isn't fair to expect 'in sickness and in health' to include an in-law's as well, so don't make unreasonable demands, whatever your expectations may be. Ideally, you'd like your partner to share everything with you, the worrying and the caring, but don't take it for granted.

Norah's story

Cancerous cells had spread into Norah's lymphatic system and her liver and bones were found to be affected. The oncologist spelled out the possibilities for treatment, but avoided any mention of the future. "I knew this was the beginning of the end," says Sally. "I didn't need to be told, but I was frightened for Mum. She was already in quite a lot of pain and I was desperate to stop it getting any worse. All my questions were about pain relief and the control of pain. I knew from what had, and what mostly hadn't, been said that there was no chance of Mum getting better."

The words 'there's nothing more we can do' are, understandably, met with dread and despair. However, while it may mean that the end of the medical road has been reached as far as treatment is concerned, it doesn't mean that care and support are at an end. Ofcaps must now concentrate on enhancing the quality of life, and giving practical and emotional support so that pain is eased and issues about daily living are not a concern.

Sally's already difficult routine was turned on its head while Norah was in hospital. First there was Brad, the dog, to deal with. "Fortunately his needs weren't great," says Sally, "and I persuaded the girls to take responsibility for him."

Then there was the upheaval of including in her already hectic, packed schedule a daily, or sometimes twice daily, visit to

Norah in hospital nine miles away. "I felt sick with worry all the time," says Sally. "I was permanently exhausted but only I could deal with that. Mum was the one with the biggest problem and I felt so helpless and so sad for her. Seeing her there in that ward, among a crowd of strangers – it seemed quite wrong. She looked so vulnerable and pathetic. She cried a lot, too, because she was very frightened. There was no-one for her to speak to except me."

Norah would be in for 10 days, Sally was told. Then what? she asked. Then she's yours, your responsibility, she was told. A nurse will pop in each day to change her dressing, they added, implying that this big favour would solve everything and enable Sally, Beth and Suzy to carry on their lives as if nothing had ever happened – and as if there wasn't a terribly sick old lady a few yards away in a cottage in the garden.

Sally's frenetic life then went into overdrive. On top of her normal work routine at the school and all that that threw at her in the way of stress, brain strain and physical effort, she crammed into each day a crash course in patients' and carers' rights. This she achieved through friends, contacts, the internet, books and a neighbour who used to work for the Marie Curie Cancer Care charity, which offers care for patients in their own homes (Helpline: 020 7599 7777 **www.mariecurie.org.uk**).

"One of the first things I learnt was not to allow my mother to be discharged from hospital until I was ready for her, with everything in place for her at home," Sally says. "I refused to be bullied or humiliated into bringing her back before everything was ready, however hard they tried to persuade me.

"One senior nurse became quite spiteful by implying that Mum was preventing someone else in greater need from having her hospital bed. But I dug my heels in and I'm so glad I did because by the time Mum came home she was feeling a little stronger. It was a week after she was meant to have left and I had a proper system set up that would ensure she was well looked after."

It is usual for a 'care package' to be in place by the time a patient leaves hospital, so that their GP, hospice team and Macmillan nurses are all aware of the situation and in a position to react.

Just being out of hospital and knowing that treatment, often with its unpleasant side effects, has ended, can lift the mood of some cancer patients, especially those who have come to terms with their condition.

Through the willingness of friends and neighbours to be volunteers, and augmented by paid professional carers, Sally was able to draft a timetable of Mum-sitters who would spend up to a couple of hours each in the garden cottage with Norah.

It was an ideal solution to a very tricky problem. But it was only a solution as long as it worked, and there were many times when Sally was telephoned in the morning, just as she was leaving for school, by a well-intentioned friend who was booked in to do a shift that day saying she was sorry but she couldn't make it after all.

"There were so many occasions when I just wanted burst into tears," says Sally. "But I couldn't. I had to go on, and that usually meant leaning on someone who was already doing far more than their fair share. You learn who your friends are – they're the ones who really do mean it when they urge you to call them if you ever need anything."

Sally took on the night shift herself. Between 8pm and 8am she was responsible for Norah's welfare, a daunting and worrying task that reduced her sleeping hours from a previously comfortable eight to a fitful, edgy, four or five – not enough for her to go on in this punishing routine indefinitely. A baby alarm rigged up between her house and Norah's bedroom gave a certain peace of mind, but Sally never felt able to relax and would sometimes go and sit with her mother in the small hours, just to be near her and to know she was safe and sleeping soundly.

"I was existing in a sort of parallel world at this point," she says. "I was utterly, totally exhausted the whole time. I don't know what kept me going – maybe just knowing that there was no-one else to do it, but maybe I was partly fuelled by anger, too, for the unfairness of our situation. And, of course, I couldn't let Mum down."

Sally says she felt guilty for having the thought, but she needed to find out how long Norah was likely to live. "The strain was almost unbearable but I felt that if I knew it wasn't going to go on indefinitely, then I'd probably manage better," she says.

"I'd been warned by friends that it could be difficult to get a prognosis, and personally I thought I'd have problems because I'd put so many backs up over the months. I could imagine phones being put down on me or doors being firmly closed as soon as I gave my name. 'Oh, it's that woman – now's our chance to get our revenge against that hysterical meddler.' But I was amazed at how easy it was."

At first Sally was told that no-one knew how long Norah would live and no-one was willing to make a calculated guess. She persisted and finally found a doctor who answered her question: "If it was your mother who was as ill as this, how long would you give her?" Probably another four to six months, came the reply. Sally decided not to tell Beth and Suzy until nearer the end, although they were aware that their Grandma was terminally ill.

'How long until the end?' is the question that people may want the answer to but which few people in authority willingly commit themselves to with any degree of certainty. Doctors genuinely want to be helpful and honest, but putting a time span on such an imponderable can be very much a shot in the dark. Everyone is affected differently and responds to treatment in different ways, even if they have a number of things in common, such as age, type of cancer and extent of the disease. Survival can be influenced by fitness, willpower and the avoidance (or development) of complications.

With so many uncertainties, most doctors will say that the best they can give is an educated guess based on average figures.

Even having a guestimate can help Ofcaps to start coming to terms with the situation and the future. But do bear in mind that a doctor's advice can only be a guide to what might happen and not an accurate forecast of what will happen.

May's story

One day May was a fully functioning human being, the next – literally at a stroke – she'd had much of the life snuffed out of her. After coping with the initial horror of what had happened, it was clear to Douglas, his wife Carol and his brother, Hugh, newly arrived at May's bedside from France, that it was astonishing how she had survived. Mentally, May was rather like an open door, Carol says. "You could see inside a little way, but you weren't sure what was in there."

But the frail patient certainly had a voice, which she exercised to alarming effect, as those within earshot discovered when she came round after her stroke. Her first words were a string of juicy expletives, including several exclamations of 'fuck!' – a word her family were sure had never passed her lips before.

The speech problem was embarrassing at first and everyone

would try to shush her, but they soon learnt they were wasting their time. It was particularly difficult for visitors in the early days when, while they were making small talk, May would suddenly unleash a tirade of 'f-words' at them.

Stroke is the largest single cause of disability in the UK, with more than 300,000 affected at any one time. Roughly a third recover, a third die within the first year and a third are left with serious disabilities, most commonly affecting mobility. About a fifth of stroke survivors suffer catastrophic reactions of aggressive swearing or similarly inappropriate social behaviour, which is particularly upsetting to them and their families.

Recovery of the affected area of the brain is sometimes possible over varying periods of time. Unbridled swearing is a symptom of dysphasia, which is defined as 'impairment in communication' or, more profoundly, 'the loss of all understanding or use of language'. Because swearing is built in at the biological level, dysphasics frequently retain the bluest of words, which they use with impunity, often adding stress to give different meanings.

May was paralysed down her left side, rendering her immobile and bed bound. Seven weeks after her stroke, when there were pitifully few signs to encourage Douglas and Carol to think that a recovery into independence would be likely, they decided they had to get her out of the hospital.

They feared that as long as she was still in there, she was unlikely to make any significant progress. She needed physiotherapy, for a start. The hospital had promised them that this would happen. It didn't – at least not in the way they'd been led to expect. May was hauled out and given ten minutes of a promised first half-hour of physio 12 days after her stroke, and that was it. Enquiries were met with non-committal responses and frequent references to staff shortages. On one occasion, Douglas was brushed off with an unthinking "Your mother is 94 you know, so it's unlikely anything could make a difference to her now."

Disillusioned and upset, and urged on by the fear that May ran the risk of becoming institutionalised if she stayed in hospital much longer, Douglas and Carol set about planning her return home. It wasn't easy, but by taking advice from The Stroke Association (0845 3033 100 **www.stroke.org.uk**) and using the services of a home nursing agency, they managed to get May out.

Anyone who stays in hospital for more than a few weeks is liable to suffer to some degree from any or, in the worst cases, possibly all of these symptoms of institutionalisation:

- Mental stagnation
- Loss of self-esteem
- Apathy
- Lethargy
- Disinterest
- Demoralisation

- Loss of appetite
- Lack of care about appearance
- Loss of dignity

Ofcaps can help Mum or Dad avoid sinking into a trough of listlessness by arranging an appointment with the hospital's visiting hairdresser or even an aromatherapist as a means of lifting their spirits (yes, even for Dad), organising changes of clothing, talking about events outside in the real world, in fact initiating anything that will stimulate their minds and help them focus on situations other than their current predicament.

One source of inspiration could be the voluntary organisation that supports pastoral areas of life in many hospitals. Usually called the League of Friends, it not only fundraises but runs invaluable services for patients such as the book trolley. Seek advice from the Friends about what comforts are available to medium and long stay patients.

It was at this stage that the many well thought out features of May's sheltered accommodation came into their own. A friend of Carol's, a newly retired occupational therapist, took a careful look at the flat and advised on what specialised equipment, including a multi-functional bed, would be of benefit. No-one could give any clue about how long the arrangements would have to continue. May's GP was non-committal, the stroke specialist warned against over optimism but thought there was a good chance of at least partial mobility and speech returning, and Carol and Douglas looked no further ahead than a day at a time.

Some feeling and movement had returned to May's left side, but there was still no question of her being able to live without total care. A physiotherapist came in three times a week. It was an expensive commitment but worth it, the Ofcaps felt, because of the effect it was having. With her recovering speech, May expressed her feelings quite clearly about her physical limitations.

Carol wanted above all to make sure her mother-in-law was comfortable. "It upset me that here was someone who had been so physically capable, so independent, and now she needed help in every aspect of her life. I wasn't always sure the care workers were as aware of her needs as they might have been.

"I often had the impression they would do the minimum and weren't tuned in well enough to her situation. I think this was mostly to do with the fact that we couldn't get a proper rota going because the agency was struggling to recruit enough care workers. So we'd have the same nice couple of women for three or four days, then we wouldn't see them for three weeks, and in the meantime there'd be an assortment of others, some of whom would come perhaps once and then never return. It was difficult for them, unsettling for May and annoying for all of us."

The shortage of care workers is well documented and many agencies recruit from overseas to make up the shortfall. The main reason for the shortage is poor pay. They can earn more by stacking supermarket shelves, says one carer support worker. And the sort of work they're expected to do requires them sometimes to live-in, which is impractical if they have a family, and almost always to run a car, which they can rarely afford to do.

Trained carers with good language skills are attracted from countries such as Poland and Zimbabwe by the abundance of work opportunities and the salaries that compare favourably with what they'd be paid at home. As live in care workers, too, they have a roof over their heads.

Douglas's medium term plan for his mother's care was to employ agency carers. But at about £500 a week, it was much the same as the cost of a place in a home and it was this discovery, together with concern about the massive drain on May's finances, that caused him to start investigating a new plan of action. This would involve moving May into a nursing home and selling her flat to fund the cost. There should be enough money from the property sale, he told Carol, to keep his mother in a home even if she lived to be well over 100.

In the meantime, anxious to put an even tenor into his mother's life, Douglas searched the internet and, after several days of concerted emailing and taking up of references, he secured the services of a Polish woman in her early forties. Marta, with a winning smile and a good grasp of English, took up residence in May's flat and set about her new duties with enthusiasm and efficiency.

Although the Ofcaps admit they felt May had probably made as much progress as she was ever going to, they were impressed with the way she responded to Marta's efforts. Marta continued with the physiotherapy routine, meaning the physio no longer needed to call, and May's speech was now coherent enough for those familiar with it to understand her. Her mobility was still severely impaired and she remained very ill, with the ever present risk of a further stroke, but there was an energy about Marta that percolated through to May and stopped her feeling so much of an invalid.

Many stroke patients suffer depression but May remained upbeat, if not exactly her former cheery self. With the changed atmosphere after Marta's arrival, there was a buzz about the flat and both Douglas and Carol felt their despair lifting, too.

Rehabilitation after a stroke can be greatly helped by Mum or Dad's attitude and by the attitude of those around them. Depending on the severity of its effect, mental and physical stimulation play a vital part in recovery and the restoration of morale.

It's likely to be hard work. Encouraging Mum or Dad to take an interest in life again involves a lot more than just sitting them in front of the television, tempting though that may be. It could take the best part of a day to get them and their wheelchair and all the necessary accoutrements out to the local stroke club and back home again, but the rewards will make it worthwhile. Contact with others in a similar situation is beneficial and a great means of picking up survival hints and tips, and the outing will provide conversational fodder right round to the time of the next trip.

You need to be sensitive to the fact that visitors may be awkward or embarrassed about seeing Mum or Dad in a paralysed state, so be sure to prepare them, suggest kindly that they don't speak to them as though they are a child, and encourage them to keep coming to call. It's easy to turn into a recluse after such a life-changing event as a stroke, so you need to help reduce the obstacles to the outside world. Do this by taking advice from wherever you can get it: hospitals, GPs, practice nurses, occupational therapists, The Stroke Association, other stroke patients and their carers – and observe how others manage whenever you are in their company.

With no specific nursing skills, other than those learned by instinct while bringing up her family, Carol says she felt 'awed but not overwhelmed' by the responsibility of caring for May when Marta had time off. Her biggest concern, she says, was the delicate matter of May's personal hygiene. "Frankly, when you've changed nappies as many times as I have as a mother, and you've dealt with horses and litters of puppies, you don't tend to blanch, much, when mopping up pee and poo. But this was different. This was my mother-in-law – not a blood relative, but Douglas's beloved Mother, reduced to virtual helplessness and reliance on the compassion of others."

So how did Carol overcome this difficulty? "I asked an old friend of mine who'd trained as a nurse years ago. She advised me there's no point being tentative and wishing you had a dozen clothes pegs on your nose. You just treat it like any other chore that has to be got through, develop a routine so that you have everything to hand when the time comes, and once you've done it the first time it becomes easier. And it's true, it does – it just isn't very nice. But then, it isn't exactly a bundle of fun for the owner of the bottom."

The inability to care for their own personal hygiene is one of the many upsetting aspects of the diseases and disabilities that afflict older people. Just because someone is rendered immobile doesn't mean their hair stops growing, their nails don't need trimming or their skin doesn't need looking after.

Being confined to bed means that much of what a woman considers her normal regimen must go by the board. Be aware that no average NHS establishment includes a 'cleanse, tone, moisturise' routine in its morning and evening cat's-lick-wash procedure. This is where Ofcaps come in, bulging washbags and vanity cases at the ready, to spruce Mum up and make her feel lovely and loved.

One thing that might stop most of the family in their tracks when they see Mum propped up on her pillows is the terrible realisation: 'Oh my God, she's grown a beard.' Sadly, it is true that neglect of the beauty routine, combined with some medication, can result in something to rival Santa Claus's facial fungus. Basically, deal with it, or get it dealt with.

If Mum knew she'd gone beyond the prickly hedgehog stage and the grandchildren were too terrified to come through the door for fear they might have to kiss her, she'd grab the nearest electric hedge trimmer if only she could reach it. So do her a favour, tackle the delicate subject and eradicate the fuzz. If you don't know what to do, consult a beautician or a sympathetic soul at Boots.

Jack's story

Jack's health deteriorated because of his drinking habits. Without being watched 24 hours a day he was at great risk, says his daughter, Jenny. Wherever she turned, and whoever she sought help from, not one person among all the health professionals and social services personnel she saw considered he – or she – needed help.

"I understand how hard it is for them to try and react to everyone's needs," Jenny says, "but they couldn't seem to see my problems or take me seriously. Not one person thought Dad had a drink problem. They obviously thought it was just a case of a slightly eccentric old man indulging in a tot too much. My guess is that he was suffering from depression and that, to an extent, was what caused him to drink.

"He spent a lot of money in the pub on himself and a lot on other people. He was taken advantage of, I know that, but he wouldn't listen when I urged him not to keep buying drinks for hangers-on and strangers. He was known as a jolly, affable character and was very popular, but people didn't see him as I saw him."

Concern about Jack's profligate spending encouraged Jenny to secure enduring power of attorney for herself and her sister after one of their father's stays in hospital. She felt it was important that they had control of his finances at a time when he seemed quite heedless of the consequences of his actions.

Arrangements for an enduring power of attorney need to be made by Ofcaps while their parent is still *compos mentis*. Sooner rather than later is very much the preferred option or the procedure becomes complicated and, because it involves a solicitor, even more expensive.

By all means shop around for the best price. Expect to pay anything from about £75.

However, be warned that even when an Ofcap has enduring power of attorney its powers are extremely limited and its operation is severely constrained to prevent fraud. This means that, for example, if your Mum has been assessed and registered as mentally disabled, you need to:

- Register with the court (£220) to be able to encash investments

- Seek the court's approval (£515, which includes a solicitor's fee) if, for example, you need to sell Mum's house to fund her nursing home fees

Bear in mind, too, that apart from the costs involved, the time it takes to set everything in motion is considerable.

Before you deal with the enduring power of attorney issue, take the opportunity to ensure that Mum or Dad's will is in order and to sort out bank, pension and insurance details as well as any inheritance tax planning.

Enduring power of attorney helpline: 0845 330 2963
www.guardianship.gov.uk.

Jack's hopelessness with money was taken advantage of by a woman from a care agency who came each Thursday to collect a list and do his shopping. She would ask him to write cheques made out to her for shopping that she hadn't done, but he had no idea what he was doing, mainly because he was clueless about handling housekeeping money but also because his mind was constantly fuddled with drink. Jenny also suspected that the 'carer' was sneaking the odd £10 or £20 from the drawer in the kitchen table where Jack kept his pension money. When her suspicion grew to certainty she had to decide whether to go to the police, who would help her lay a trap for definitive proof to be established, or just report the matter to the care agency.

While she wanted the woman to be caught and stopped, she simply didn't have the stamina to pursue the case. She complained to the agency and learnt later that the woman was found to have been doing the same thing in other households. A court case followed and the woman was banned from working as a carer again.

After this episode, Jenny took over paying all Jack's bills for him because, as she says, he couldn't be trusted to handle anything.

Although Jack was not deemed to have any medical need to be in a home or in a nursing home Jenny knew he needed more supervision because he was becoming increasingly vulnerable. What with his falls, his lack of mobility, the problems caused by his drunkenness and his lack of interest in looking after himself, he was presenting a very sorry case.

Jenny bore the burden on her own as her sister, several years older, lived 150 miles away and showed no interest in sharing the responsibility. "I feel a bit resentful that it all fell on me," says Jenny. "She played no part at all in anything to do with Dad. I suppose everyone's different and we all have our reasons for doing what we do, or don't do, and she obviously never felt the same way as I did about our duty to Dad and what Mum would have expected.

"When Dad was laid up, recovering at our house from one of his frequent chest infections, I paid for care for him once a day, which was all I could afford. Someone came in from a care agency to make sure he was up, had his breakfast and took his tablets. Twice a week someone came in to give him a bath but he would usually tell them he didn't want a bath. The care worker would say OK and then tell me that there was nothing she could do to make him have one. So I would be paying £8 for him to have a bath which he never had, even though he always told me he did."

Jack's increasingly desperate plight forced Jenny into a decision. "There was only one solution," she says, "and that was for Dad to come and live with us. He said he'd had enough of living on his own and when I said he could be with us permanently he seemed quite happy about it."

Jenny's husband and two sons, who by now were aged 16 and 20, were not wildly enthusiastic, especially as it was going to mean moving house. "It was a lot to ask of the family, I know," Jenny says. "We'd all coped OK before because we'd always known Dad's stays were not for ever and he'd be going back to his own place. This was going to be different.

"My children had been reasonably tolerant about Dad and his difficulties because he wasn't under our roof. They got a bit fed up with it all but they weren't close to him. My father's never been a sort of Grandpa figure to them. In fact, he was never very interested in them at all. He was interested in himself, not anyone else in the family."

The house move, to a neighbouring village, was to a bigger place complete with self-contained ground-floor accommodation for Jack. There was even space inside for his mobility scooter – his last link with independence. While he bought a final round of drinks at his local in town, Jenny's family braced themselves for his arrival and the next stage of their lives.

Preparing a home for a disabled person to live in involves an inspection and assessment by social services. An occupational therapist will advise on what will be needed – but, be warned, get your requests for equipment in early, well before Mum or Dad is coming home, and don't expect it all to come free.

Difficulties arise if there are strict criteria or long waiting times. Assessment is meant to be within 48 hours of first contact with social services and to be completed within four weeks. Thereafter, equipment is meant to be provided by social services within seven days but, while everyone does their best to get things moving, there is no legal time within which the equipment must be provided.

For an NHS wheelchair, which is provided on free long term loan, the GP, hospital or social services can refer you to the wheelchair service. For other necessary equipment or alterations to the home, investigate the availability of grants and try and get as much information out of the hospital before you and your dependant are cast adrift from that safety net. Mum or Dad's former professional trade association might be disposed to give a one-off gift of £200 or so to help out a former member, as might the Royal British Legion if they used to serve in the armed forces.

Anthea's story

Kate, single since her divorce five years earlier, and with both her children grown up and living away, decided after nearly one more year of regular visiting and constant worrying that she would give up her job as a pub chef and move in with Anthea. She could do it quickly, which was important, as her accommodation went with her job and her own home was already let and being used as a vital income stream.

Kate's lost income would be offset in part, she hoped, by any allowances due to Anthea. She quickly discovered that that was a false hope and the basic attendance allowance of £40.55 a week was nothing more than a disappointing drop in the ocean. Kate applied for the carer's allowance of £45.70 but was denied it on the grounds that she had an income from letting her home. Financially, and in terms of her career, Kate's move was a bad one, but for Anthea's comfort and safety, and for the family's well-being as a whole, it was selfless and entirely good. Kate took charge of Anthea's finances and arranged to be a signatory for her pension and building society passbook. With her own life on hold for an indefinite period, Kate consulted with Bob and they agreed she should be 'paid' a modest monthly salary from her Mother's account. She was concerned about losing pension entitlement so arranged to continue paying a National Insurance contribution of about £2 a week after declaring herself a self-employed care worker.

Bob's work prevented him from being anything more than an occasional visitor, but he undertook the nuts and bolts of managing Kate's house for her in her absence, thus saving on the letting agent's fees. Bob's wife, Julie, brought their two boys to visit as often as possible, so that they might provide a link to the more recent years of Anthea's life.

What goes into our brain first lasts longest, so that someone with dementia can remember their father's name but not their grandchildren's names. They remember their parents much more than their spouse, for example, because he or she came on the scene in later life.

If an Ofcap tells Mum or Dad: 'You can't possibly be expecting me to call. I said I was coming on Wednesday and it's only Tuesday now,' it means nothing to them. Remember: they're living with no logic at all, or at least with a distorted logic, and that can be pretty frightening.

Grandchildren can be alarmed by dementia and they need to have it explained to them. They may think Grandma doesn't love them because she doesn't know their name or becomes impatient with them. Try and help them see that this is an illness and talk about Grandma positively to them. Focus on what she achieved, not on what she can no longer do, so that they maintain their respect.

One of the really hard things about caring for someone with dementia is that Mum or Dad looks more or less like they used to, but you can't see what's going on inside their brain. If the loss of brain cells was manifested physically it would make the decline more obvious and more easy to cope with. This only happens later, when they move with a sort of shuffling gait.

Kate says she was terrified of her carer's role at first, and terrified for her Mother, too. "I was tentative about everything because I was so scared of doing the wrong thing. So often I felt bad because I would think Mum was being bloody minded, but at least I now knew the reason.

"It explains an incident after Bob had pulled her leg about being forgetful. I followed her into her bedroom and found her crying her eyes out. When I asked what was wrong, she said 'Everyone thinks I'm stupid and silly, but I'm not'. It was awful – I felt so sorry for her."

Contact with the Alzheimer's Society (helpline: 0845 300 0336 **www.alzheimers.org.uk**) resulted in Kate taking Anthea along to dementia counselling sessions where a process of shared experiences, learning about the disease and the acquisition of coping skills instilled a measure of self-esteem and confidence that had been rapidly dwindling.

Dementia counsellors often need to glean information from the carer if the person they are counselling has limited or poor recall. It is worth Ofcaps remembering that people with dementia can often do more than is expected of them. A dementia counsellor says: "We don't always recognise how much they can do. We certainly don't recognise the pain that they are in. If we isolate them more then they will become depressed and do less well.

"It is my aim to make people with dementia feel as good as they can about themselves within the limits of what's going on. Counselling is recognising the problem, helping them to see that the problem is beyond their control. You can adjust to wearing spectacles, for instance, but with memory loss, we are embarrassed.

"Certain parts of our personality accept some loss quite happily, such as the loss we have of muscles in our eyes, but we are really much more embarrassed about the muscles in our brain going wrong. Dementia is as physical as that. What's needed is spectacles for the mind. I say don't blame yourself, blame your neurotransmitters (chemical messengers). If you know it's not something to do with you, then it's not quite as bad."

Although it didn't come as a huge shock to Bob and Kate when they learned Anthea had Alzheimer's, they did find it difficult to understand what was going on in her head. Kate, living with her full time now, says it was impossible to tell how much she knew about her situation. "At first things were sometimes almost normal and like the old days," she says, "but within a year of the diagnosis, by the time I moved in with her, I could see she was starting to change a lot, becoming more isolated."

Within about nine months of leaving her demanding job of cooking meals in a gastropub, Kate was flung into a routine of caring for Anthea that she says made her former busy life seem like a holiday. "I very soon learnt that I couldn't leave Mum for longer than half an hour for fear of what harm she might do to herself," she says.

"By the time her short term memory had completely gone I knew that if, for example, I gave her a cup of tea, she would forget to drink it. If she ventured into the kitchen to warm up her cold tea – in a saucepan, no less – she would forget it was on the stove, or forget how to turn the stove off. It's always very difficult to get her to take any medication for anything – the pills, including Aricept, which she is meant to take in the morning are often found swilling about in the dregs of tea in her cup.

"She can dress herself – although I have to check she has her pants on – but the combination of clothes tends to be a little strange sometimes. I once took her out for a pub lunch and she insisted on wearing her bed jacket. It's a long-running battle to get her to wear suitable clothes in the right order. I help her with them but they still go a bit wrong. She has a habit of walking round with her stockings round her ankles, Nora Batty style, so she often ends up wearing socks instead.

"Mum can go nowhere on her own, can't count out money, can't shop, sometimes forgets how to use the phone and refuses to wear an alarm round her neck. She is short-sighted but will rarely wear her specs. Her ears are as sharp as a radar station. She has no concentration, cannot follow a TV programme, spends hours looking at the newspaper but remembers absolutely nothing of what she has read, but it does make her look as though she is doing something, and she likes that. She likes me to think she's busy and occupied. She used to love doing housework – now she contents herself with moving all the towels into the dining room, or putting the salt cellar in the bathroom."

Routine will help reinforce what Mum or Dad is trying to do, and distraction will take away the pain of when they are failing to do what they're trying to do. People with dementia can become quite obsessive.

By all means start by getting Mum or Dad to write notes to themselves: 'Close the door' is a good one for peace of mind, and suggest they put a checklist by the telephone so that when they answer a call they know what to ask to ascertain who is speaking and what they want.

In time, though, their spatial awareness will go so that tasks such as putting the oven on are beyond them and they don't understand how it works. Ofcaps who are alarmed to find a newly widowed parent in this situation need to be aware that the now departed spouse will have been doing some valiant covering up over the past months or years. Widowhood brings a terrifying exposure to the world, where shelter and protection are no longer there on a daily basis.

Beware introducing change.

- Any item in the home should always be replaced by something they've always had and that's familiar to them
- The kettle should be the same shape
- Keys should be the same type
- Everything should help the memory

Salutary tales include the Ofcap who thoughtfully removed Mum's grotty old gas kettle and replaced it with a shiny electric one. What does Mum do? She puts it on the gas stove, because that's what she has always done with her kettle.

Here's another one. The Ofcap wants to make Mum's life easier so installs a microwave oven on the kitchen worktop. Hours of patient instruction follow, but Mum isn't able to tell you that new learning is one thing you can't do with dementia. Did her Ofcap say something about foil and microwave ovens? Mum uses foil for her oven cooking, so into the microwave goes the foil covered dish. And Mum's always cooked food in the oven for 90 minutes, so round goes the microwave timer to 90 minutes. As you can see, risk can come into the home hand-in-hand with kind gestures.

Kate works entirely to a routine, hoping this brings at least some order and comfort to her now seriously confused mother. "It is a full time job physically looking after Anthea," she says, "and trying out different things to stimulate the last remaining brain cells.

"You have to be canny, one step ahead to avoid situations that give her grief. We seem to get equal pleasure out of our achievements. I sat her down with a Next Home catalogue and set her the task of choosing new curtains. This took most of the day as she couldn't remember what she was supposed to be doing – but she did it, and she felt so pleased with herself.

"She can knit, after a fashion, so I've encouraged her to knit some squares so we can make a blanket for charity. I label everything so she knows what's what, but she still makes a mess of everything, which really doesn't matter. She drops stitches, forgets where she is with a certain row, forgets all the time what she is knitting, produces peculiar offerings of squares of a multitude of stitches – but she does it! It is the first time in probably two years or so that I have seen her voluntarily do something creative which isn't just moving the bathroom things around or plastering her face in make-up and brushing her hair."

Incontinence pads present a continuing challenge, although the situation has improved since the first half-dozen times when a bemused Anthea, not recognising what they were and not remembering what she'd been told to do, secreted used ones in a drawer. Another time, she popped one in the oven to dry. Because she had no idea what the things were for, she didn't know how to cope with them. Kate solved the problem by an ingenious method of colour association: she helps Anthea put used pads into a bucket whose lid and sides she has decorated with flower shapes cut out from the plastic bags in which the pads are sold.

Kate carves out an hour each day for herself in the morning and an hour in the evening for exercise. "In this situation you crave life," she says. "I walk near the beautiful houses which surround the park, imagining people getting ready for going out for the evening, talking about the day's events, planning for the future.

"It's a pretty lonely existence as I'm locked into a situation of living at the pace of an Alzheimer's patient, a pace like no-one else's. Everything happens very slowly, usually by negotiation, if it happens at all. My whole being is concentrated on Mum. It's incredibly tiring. I feel drained at the end of every day. Utterly shattered.

"She shouts at me a lot, which I used to find really upsetting but which I've now learned to try and ignore. I do a lot of jaw clenching. Sometimes it's like dealing with a naughty and bad tempered very old baby. Her moods are ferocious – she'll scream at me in public, using swear words I didn't know she knew.

"She gets furious with me if I'm taking her to an appointment with the optician or the chiropodist. She'll glower in a silent rage all the way there, sinking lower and lower into the passenger seat so there's just a cloud of fury above her little old grey head, but is then sweetness and charm when she arrives, twinkling outrageously at the staff."

If you can understand what Mum or Dad's doing and why they are doing it, it will defuse some of your frustration, suggests an Alzheimer's counsellor. Your role change means a life change, which necessitates an enormous adjustment.

You have to come to terms with the fact Mum or Dad is there in person but has a totally dependent role and is unable to make choices for themselves. It is very painful when you see the man or woman who has taught you such a lot needing so much care and support. It's also embarrassing because people don't always see your parent as the erudite and clever person they once were. They see them, quite possibly, as a shuffling imbecile, which is very sad.

According to Kate, the local doctor seems to do nothing except go on holiday, but Anthea will not hear a word against him. She still steadfastly refuses to acknowledge there is anything wrong with her and kicks up a massive fuss if anything occurs out of the ordinary.

"It can be soul-destroying explaining and repeating everything, time and again," says Kate. "All the books on caring tell you what to do, but none tell you that it is frustrating, irritating and impossible to carry on your own life. The most difficult thing as a carer is that, in spite of being told to do loads of life-enhancing activities for the person you're caring for, there just isn't the time to do them because of trying to keep day-to-day life together."

Kate finds the radio a godsend in her efforts to keep Anthea interested and distracted from her incessant chatter about her childhood. A favourite programme is Loose Ends. "My choice for her, rather appropriately," says Kate. "To be honest I'll do just about anything to keep her off the childhood subject. It's like a soundtrack stuck on repeat."

Anthea doesn't like people coming to the house. She makes the excuse of having a cold, not understanding that it isn't a cold but a side effect of Aricept. She will occasionally visit friends, but has no recollection of the occasion by the time she reaches home. They're good to her, Kate says, and treat her with great sympathy. "I sometimes get them to come round, not too many at a time, even if Mum's said she doesn't want to see them. It's important to keep some semblance of normality, after all, and Mum's friends always used to be important to her."

Kate's morning hour for herself, when Anthea is safely in bed listening (or probably not listening, Kate suspects) to the radio, gives her time to keep the rest of the family up to date with the situation. She also likes to communicate with Anthea's friends who live too far away for visits. She has asked them all to send picture postcards frequently because they give hours of pleasure to Anthea, who enjoys looking at the pictures and talking about them with Kate.

Outings with Anthea are generally a mix of pain and pleasure for Kate, with the added frisson of unpredictability keeping her ever alert. A favourite destination is the local garden centre – "such an important social service" is how she describes it, gratefully. It offers convenient parking, plenty to look at, a café, toilets, bits and pieces to buy, some distracting muzak, free admission and, importantly, it's all on one level. A trip there is always popular.

CHAPTER 5

Closing scenes

A tremulous little voice wakes her in the small hours. It is a cry for help, slightly tinny and distorted because it is reaching her sleepy head through a baby alarm. She forces herself awake and slips into the familiar routine: down the stairs, out of the back door, across the garden at the side of the house, in through another front door, across the hall, into a dimly-lit bedroom. She half lifts, half pulls a small body out of its bed and sets it on its pot. They exchange a little mumbled banter, ending with a silly rendition of 'Tinkle, tinkle, little star', which puts a smile on their faces. Deep down, though, they don't really like to acknowledge that this is happening, at this hour, in the night – again.

She puts her mother back into her bed, makes her comfortable, and creeps back to her own.

Nearly half a century ago it was Sally who needed her Mother's help to save her from wetting the bed. It was Mother who was so adept at patting her clean and dry and pulling up her pants. Now Sally does that for her, but she receives no thanks. She wouldn't expect to – it's what Mother did, now it's what she does.

The role reversal is complete. Now Mother is the trusting toddler and the structure of her life, her very existence, is down to Sally, her nearest and her very dearest.

Everyone hopes that they'll stay in their own home for the rest of their lives. They dread the prospect of hospitals or care homes and place their trust in a mercifully swift death. Anything slow and lingering doesn't bear thinking about.

The best thing, they agree, would be to slip away quietly in their sleep, with no fuss. And most of all, they say they don't want to be a burden to anyone, especially their families. Unfortunately, this is one aspect that is beyond their control. Once they become totally dependent it isn't always possible for an older person to be able to dictate the way their future should unfold.

For Ofcaps, decisions about life and death and the sometimes long, costly, upsetting stage in between, are stressful and way beyond anything in their experience. Understandably, they can't bear the thought of Mum or Dad suffering pain or being unable to indicate their distress. They are torn between thoughts of them 'needing to die' and 'keeping them alive at all costs', so they place their faith in doctors as life nears its end. In unknown territory it's best to be led by someone who knows the way.

Being faced with what is, literally, a life or death dilemma is the unhappiest of situations but in some cases it can be solved by invoking the terms of a living will, if your parent has made one. If they haven't, bear in mind that the wishes of the family, whatever they may be, carry no weight with the medical profession – only the witnessed, written, formal wishes of the patient can be considered.

A living will can enable Mum or Dad to make their decisions and choices known regarding medical treatment should they suffer loss of mental capacity through serious illness. It is usually a written document explaining the circumstances under which the person would not want to receive life-prolonging medical treatment, meaning that clinical staff and others are aware of their wishes when they are unable to communicate with them in any other way. As a result, Ofcaps are not left with difficult decisions, unsure what their parent might have wanted.

Be prepared for it not to be as clear cut as that. Sometimes a living will can be quite useless, however definite your Mum or Dad's wishes may have been, because there are questions about the legality of who can advise the medical team about the ill person's wishes. The medical profession is bound by its code of ethics not to do anything that would prevent someone living longer. It is a very difficult situation, but there is a greater chance of a living will 'working' if the family are in agreement and as many medical personnel as possible are 'on side'.

Norah's story

Knowing that Norah was unlikely to last beyond her 79th birthday in six months' time gave Sally the impetus she needed to keep going and to make the time remaining as positive as possible. "I felt strangely empowered," she says. "It's odd, but I was now armed with the knowledge I needed to see Mum's life through to its natural conclusion. It did seem possible, after all, that I was going to be able to do the right thing by her, and that made me feel better."

Norah's carers ensure she is kept comfortable and pain free, helping her change her position every couple of hours to prevent stiffness and sore skin and relaxing her by playing tapes of her favourite choral music. One carer, a qualified masseur, calls in almost every day on her way home from work to give Norah a gentle massage of her back, feet or hands, and everyone plays their invaluable individual role in raising her spirits through being a cheerful presence.

Although Norah is becoming increasingly frail, she enjoys being taken out in her wheelchair. For Sally, this is a poignant reprise of the final months of her husband's life: the family operating in slow time, everything taking twice or even three times as long as it normally would. Even a trip to the supermarket takes hours, what with the wheelchair having to come along too, and Norah needing to be put in and out of the passenger seat with the utmost care.

Sally tries to involve Norah in the shopping, too, so that she doesn't feel she is just being brought along for the ride but is actually having a useful input. With the list on a clipboard, Norah uses a thick felt-tip pen to tick off items as they go into the trolley and she jogs Sally's memory when she thinks there's a danger of things being forgotten.

In the first few weeks of Norah being at home she had to attend clinics, so Sally took occasional half-days off work to take her. "That added to my guilt and stress," she says, "because colleagues were having to cover for me in my absence and I didn't have time to return the favour."

On one clinic visit during half-term she asked Beth and Suzy to come with her and help their Granny. "It was a salutary experience for them," Sally says. "I'm glad I did it because they were able to see for themselves what a hoo-ha it is, all that physical effort of getting Mum there on time, the hanging around, the strange sadness of it all, and then the whole business in reverse to get Mum back home again. I think it did them good and it certainly helped me to share it."

Sally laughed when someone suggested she should go away for a holiday. How can I go away when my Mother is dying, and when her world is revolving around me? she asked. She was firmly told that a break would be in her best interests, and probably Norah's, indirectly, and that it would enable her to get through the coming months. "It was an appealing prospect, and not just to discover if I really was indispensable," she says.

This was when Norah's local hospice stepped in. The district nurse and the Macmillan nurse (helpline 0808 808 2020 **www.macmillan.org.uk**), both regulars now at the garden cottage, made the whole plan seem so appealing that neither Sally nor Norah could see any reason to delay. So for five days Norah went for what she called her 'hospice holiday' and Sally and the girls went on the train to stay with friends in North Wales.

Hospices specialise in the care of people living and dying with chronic illness. They also support the patient and their family. Their philosophy is neither to hasten nor to postpone death but to enable terminally ill people to live in physical comfort and die with dignity and without pain. People often go into hospices for short periods for their symptoms to be monitored or to give their carer a break (respite care).

The late Dame Cicely Saunders, the leading figure in the founding of the modern hospice movement, said: "You matter because you are you, and you matter to the end of your life."

The few days away worked a treat for Sally, who says she was made to feel even better when she collected Norah from the hospice and found that she'd been happy, too, and had enjoyed the experience. It was the breakthrough in the situation that both had really needed.

"I don't know what I'd have done if Mum had had a bad experience," Sally says. "I really don't think I could have gone on much longer without the help of the hospice. In fact Mum absolutely loved it. She's always happy to go to the hospice. She's been a couple of times since – for long weekends – and it's made all the difference in the world to me. They're wonderful to her in there and I can relax and know that she's having the best possible care. It takes some of the guilt and a lot of the worry away."

Because of the good relationship Norah has with the hospice, Sally has no qualms about her dying there. "I think all things considered, it would probably be best if she moved back in there at the end," she says. "It's a very special place – for a very special Mum."

Joan's story

In the last six months before she died, Joan was taken into hospital two or three times, but on the last occasion Helen had to 'kidnap' her and take her home because she could see the nursing staff were getting their own back on the crotchety old lady by ignoring her. Joan's response to having her demands ignored was to cry, pitifully and endlessly, so that her health started going downhill fast. "I knew I had to get her out and back to her own home," says Helen.

"She was ready to die. She'd fought long enough and now she embraced the prospect of her death. She maintained her great sense of humour to the end, and we had some great laughs together on the way. There were so many, many, good bits and we did manage to have some fun, but there were some terrible times, too. It's such a shame that in the last three years she was so difficult because it could have been such a special time with us together so much."

The one hundred people who attended the memorial service for Joan heard the vicar read out a message she had dictated to him before she died. They could hear Joan's voice in the words: "I know I have been very difficult in the last few years. In fact sometimes downright impossible. But I love you all." Helen says there wasn't a dry eye in the church.

Looking back on those last traumatic three years, Helen is confident she did everything possible to make Joan's life comfortable and to keep her pledge that she would help her stay in her own home. "It cost a fortune," she admits, "but it was my pleasure and privilege to have been able to do it. I loved my Mum and she had been a wonderful Mum to me, so this was the very least I could do for her. My brother gave me a present after Mum had died to thank me for everything I had done. I was very touched.

"What we have to remember, and what still makes us smile, is that Mum could never have gone into a home anyway because they would have thrown her out. No institution would have put up with her, that's certain."

Jack's story

Jack's new quarters in the home of daughter Jenny and her family were luxurious compared with the sheltered flat he'd just left. He was pleased to find grab rails, a special shower and an adjustable easy chair among the range of aids installed for him.

As this was a new home for all of them, it was a period of considerable adjustment, not least for Neil, Jenny's youngest son, who was about to take his GCSEs and whose journey to and from school was now going to involve a 35 minute walk and 20 minutes on a bus. "We were all making sacrifices," Jenny says. "We'd had a double garage with our old house, now we had no garage because of the annexe for Dad. This meant we had to park our cars outside and we had to keep all the bikes in a garden shed." The no-garage situation particularly irked Jenny's husband, Graham, while for Mark, their elder son, it was enough to cause him to leave home after only a fortnight. He had to have somewhere secure to leave his motorbike, he said, so he moved into a shared house with friends where there was a garage.

"Looking back on it, I am sure Mark used that as an excuse to get away," Jenny says. "I can't blame him. It wasn't very nice for the boys having Dad under the same roof. I really missed having Mark around. It hit me hard, this breaking up of our family, and all because of Dad."

Jack took only a few hours to settle in. That was all the time he needed to find his way round his area of the house, try out some of the gadgets and ride his mobility scooter a mile down the road to the village pub. Jenny was disappointed because she'd hoped he would be daunted by the distance and would decide to stay at home, but, as she says, "old habits die hard and if there's a pub that he thinks his scooter can reach, he'll be off there, however difficult the journey may be."

A month after the move and encouraged by the lighter evenings of early summer, Jack was staying out later and later. One night he still wasn't home by the time Jenny and Graham wanted to go to bed. Concerned, they took a torch and went up the lane. They found him lying in the hedge, one leg trapped under the scooter and the other bleeding heavily where he'd pulled it free. He was very drunk.

"I was disgusted," she says. "It was pathetic to see my father reduced to this. I couldn't feel sorry for him, I felt revulsion."

Jack was soon back in the hospital ward where he'd been a regular before his move out of town. The staff remembered him and the jokes started to flow again about Jack the Lad and his astonishing capacity for alcohol. With another broken leg – a different one this time – as well as a broken foot and three cracked ribs, Jack was in no position to return to the pub, nor to his new home.

"I have to be honest and say we're enjoying the freedom, knowing he is someone else's responsibility," Jenny says. "It's comforting to know that Dad is in a safe place, unable to go anywhere and get himself into trouble. But of course I'm worried about him, especially because the doctors are pretty sure that Dad actually had a heart attack that night we found him in the hedge. He's got a chest infection as well, and they're concerned about some polyps in his colon which they've removed and we're waiting for the biopsy results. He's in a pretty bad way – and it's really strange because with all the tubes and things that have been going in and out of his throat, it hurts him like mad to talk above a whisper. It's weird for him, of all people, to have been silenced."

His home with Jenny is still there for him, if and when he comes out of hospital, but in the meantime there are reminders of the earlier days of Jack's widowhood as Jenny finds herself preparing a daily meal for him again. She felt she had little choice but to do this when she discovered that Jack's lunch was being plonked down on a tray at the end of his hospital bed where he couldn't reach it. It would still be there hours later, untouched and unnoticed by anyone else.

"I've kicked up such a fuss but got absolutely nowhere," Jenny says. "Nobody will take responsibility for the situation and they've just closed ranks. I can't fight any more so I've given in and for the time being I'm bringing Dad his meals myself. Maybe things will get better when he's got his voice back. Maybe – but I doubt it."

Battles with authority are the very last thing a carer needs because these are times when everyone ought to be on the same side. Sadly, it isn't always so. When Ofcaps encounter any (or all) of the following:

- Hostility
- Insensitivity
- Obstructiveness
- 'Jobsworth' attitudes

they will need all their resources if they're to come out on top because they'll invariably be up against a far mightier force.

Two of the best weapons in an Ofcap's artillery are knowledge and dignity. Knowledge is vital to ensure you are on safe ground, that you know your rights, you are fully aware of the situation in the past and the present and you understand the consequences of any action – or inaction. Dignity is important because by hanging on to it in the thick of battle you will not let yourself down. An Ofcap who resorts to bad language and dirty tactics risks losing dignity and handing a moral victory to the other side.

If you want to pursue your complaint, and it can't be satisfactorily resolved by a reasonable approach to the person responsible or whoever is in charge of them, go to the Citizens Advice Bureau. They will guide and advise you on the best way forward. You could get an informal resolution through the Patient Advice and Liaison Service (PALS), which operates in every NHS trust and primary care trust, or you could use the Independent Complaints Advocacy Service (ICAS), which supports patients and their carers who have a complaint about their NHS treatment or care. Contact your nearest PALS or ICAS through your local Citizens Advice Bureau or online (**www.dh.gov.uk**). Alternatively, consult the Patients' Association, which can send you a booklet that will guide you through the complaints procedure across all areas of the NHS.

If your complaint is about social services you will need to go in the first instance to the council (local authority) which provides the service.

Don't ever be afraid to give in – with dignity, naturally. That way at least you can draw a line under it all. It's nearly always the little things that eat away at Ofcaps, the petty injustices and examples of unthinking crassness that can be so upsetting and lead to frenzied bouts of head-banging. Take a leaf out of Jenny's book: have your say, express your disappointment and frustration, and then show what you're made of – that you're a nicer person than they are.

May's story

For Douglas and Carol, there now began an initiation into a world they had barely been aware of before: the world of residential care and nursing homes. May's condition of dependence meant she would need a nursing home and, as she had more than £20,500 at her disposal, she would be liable for all the costs, which were likely to be about £2,500 a month.

"It was a tricky situation," says Douglas. "We were reasonably content with the status quo, but we knew that another stroke, if it came, would either kill Mum or leave her needing more intensive care than Marta or Carol could give her. We were therefore advised by her GP to seek out the home we'd be happiest with."

State help is generally available only to those whose assets fall short of that £20,500 threshold. In other words, it's hardly worth looking for any financial help if you own your own property. Of the half a million people currently in residential care, a third are having to pay all or most of the bill, which averages nearly £18,000 a year. Each local authority has its own charging policy, so always investigate and take advice.

Do be aware that means testing can be retrospective and heed the cautionary tale of an elderly woman who sold her house and gave the proceeds to her son and daughter-in-law to build a granny annexe for her at their home. She moved in, but the following year fell ill and needed to go into care. As she had no savings and no assets a confident claim for state financial support was made. The claim was dismissed on the grounds that the woman had recently disposed of her assets. Her son had to remortgage his home to pay for the nursing home fees.

There are alternatives to the 'mainstream' homes, like those run by charities such as Sue Ryder (020 7400 0440 **www.suerydercare.org.uk**) and it is possible Mum or Dad might meet the criteria for a coveted place in one of these.

Try consulting the Nursing Home Fees Agency for care fees funding advice (0800 99 88 33 **www.nhfa.co.uk**).

Within only a few days of starting the search for the right home for May, she suffered another stroke. "It was shattering," says Carol. "The amazing thing is that it didn't take her off, but it sent her back to square one in terms of her incapacity."

May remained in hospital for five weeks and the family could see she was depressed by this pitiful state of affairs. Marta spent a great deal of time with her, but it soon became obvious that even that close attention wasn't going to benefit the patient.

"We had to say goodbye to Marta at that point," says Carol. "It had been such a pleasure to have her in our lives, but it was unfair on everyone to keep her hanging around. So we helped her find another position, this time looking after a man in Scotland who'd also had a stroke."

A meeting at the hospital between the consultant geriatrician, senior nurses and a carer support worker on one side and Douglas and Carol on the other, resulted in the decision that May would be leaving hospital in 10 days' time and the recommendation was that she should go to a nursing home.

"From then on," Carol says, "all our thoughts and actions were focused on what we'd only been tentatively doing beforehand. We had to find a lovely place for May."

It is not surprising that the conversation in households such as Douglas and Carol's is dominated by the issue of what to do with Mother. Their lives, hitherto running along straight lines, have been violently thrown off course. The issue becomes an obsession.

- What's best?

- What would she want?
- What's it likely to cost?
- What are the implications?

Most questions are unanswerable but they get thrashed out constantly, while mounds of literature are acquired and leafed through, and anyone with any medical knowledge is quizzed.

The emotional strain is enormous. Other family matters get ignored. Nothing, it seems, is as important as the issue of doing the right thing for Mum or Dad.

The more space a problem is given, the more opportunity it has to dominate your life. Restored to its correct proportion it diminishes and is more manageable. Accord it the time and thought necessary, and reach a decision after acquiring whatever knowledge is required, but beware of letting it take over. Keep a lid on that hot topic and don't let it bubble over into every area of your family life.

Douglas and Carol asked Hugh if he'd like to join them in their search for a home for May but he assured them he had the greatest faith in their powers of sleuthing and would happily leave the task to them. "This made it easier in some respects," says Carol, "but it did put the whole burden on us. Yet again, we had to suppress our fury at his lack of involvement. There were we, worried sick and tramping round on cheerless, grey English days while he was soaking up the sun in the south of France with hardly a care in the world. Douglas was seething about his brother's thoughtlessness, too, so we allowed ourselves to rant about him once in a while, which I'm afraid to say made us feel a lot better!"

Taking soundings from others in a similar situation, or who had been similarly placed, helped narrow down the field for May's Ofcaps searching for a 'just right' nursing home. "We made notes so we didn't get confused between one home and another," Carol says. "It was a bit like house-hunting for ourselves, because your instincts play an equally important role.

"There was only one place where I had to be ultra-diplomatic and stop Douglas from walking straight out again. There was a community singing session going on in the residents' lounge that was so mournful and pathetic it made us want to weep. As Douglas said afterwards: 'Some bloody sing-song that was!'"

Here's an Ofcap's checklist for home hunting:

1 Remember it's a home you're seeking, not a recreation of your old boarding-school, young offenders' institution or that hostel in Germany where you had such fun in Year 9.

2 Listen out for how staff talk to residents and give them black marks if they treat them like toddlers.

3 Be unimpressed if a 'bloody sing-song' is the only social activity in a fortnight.

4   Be impressed by a home that offers regular exercise classes, even if your Mum or Dad can't partake.

5   The surroundings may be wonderful, with smart furnishings and acres of classy carpets, but those aren't the things that make a home. It's the residents' relationship with the staff which does that.

6   Discuss with the proprietor what your Mum or Dad's needs are likely to be and don't be deceived by unlikely claims.

7   Make sure you meet staff and other residents, but your most valuable information will come from other Ofcaps, so track some down once you have a shortlist.

8   Check out the cleanliness for acceptable standards of hygiene and the menus for knowledgeable, thoughtful planning.

9   Study the independent reports on residential and nursing homes on the internet. The Commission for Social Care Inspection makes one planned inspection visit and one unplanned, so you get a clear and honest snapshot (Helpline: 0845 015 0120 **www.csci.org.uk**).

10 Trust your gut instincts. You'll know if it's right when you walk through the front door.

With the choice finally made, Douglas went to see May in hospital and told her all about it. Although she couldn't speak to reply, she made it clear by the look in her eyes that she trusted him and was content.

"It was very sad to be moving her out of the hospital and not back into her own home," says Douglas. "I felt it was hugely significant – like the opening of her final chapter."

Bill's story

Beverley says that the prospect of Bill moving out of the family home brought huge feelings of relief, which increased the ever present feelings of guilt. "But as far as Dad was concerned I really did believe he was going to be happier," she says. "I would be going to visit him and that would be quality time for us both, which is something we needed and had missed for five years."

Bill moved in to his local Abbeyfield on a Sunday morning. "It all happened quite rapidly," says Beverley. "We got a phone call on the Thursday telling us he could move in that weekend. In a way that was good because it gave him less time to get in a state about it.

"He was so sweet, trying so hard to be brave but looking rather frail and frightened. For such a creature of routine and habit it must have been awful for him to be pitched into an entirely new environment. Things that we wouldn't even give a second thought became major issues.

"For instance – where are the light switches for when he goes to the loo in the middle of the night? What had I put away in which drawer? I kept trying to talk him through it and explain, but I could see that he just couldn't take it all in. It was too much.

"To say that I felt terrible is an understatement. But what he was going through must have been even worse. That first evening was too dreadful for words. I went home and took some of my migraine medication because I knew it would knock me out and I went straight to bed and slept.

"The guilt and anguish I felt has still not completely lifted, but I am happy to say that he is settling in, slowly but surely. It isn't something that is going to happen overnight. He is gradually building a new routine and establishing friendships with other people in the house, although nothing on the scale that I had hoped.

"If questioned, he would say that he was fine and there was no problem. It is only the rest of us who think we know best and who feel that his life could be so much fuller.

"He rings most days and of course I ring him to check he is OK. I usually visit about twice a week and go up to collect his laundry.

"Apart from me he doesn't get visitors. When he first moved in the rest of the family and a couple of friends called to see his new place, but everyone is always so busy. It's ironic that our lives are so packed and his is such a vacuum, but that is his choice.

"I feel guilty because it is very much a case of 'out of sight out of mind'. He isn't here in the house so I tend not to think about him so much and probably nobody else in the family thinks of him at all because of being so preoccupied with other things.

"I can't pretend that life here isn't much, much, easier and less stressed. It is good to have our home back, but I can't get the feeling out of my head that I have betrayed him and that I have been an utterly selfish cow.

"I think Alec thought that it would automatically resolve the problems we were having in our relationship. Dad's presence had become a convenient scapegoat, I fear. But actually the guilt I am feeling probably means that is not going to happen as easily as he thought.

"I am sure Dad will be fine and he's in the best possible place. But I am also sure that if he had known what was going to happen he would never have left his little bungalow and that given the choice of moving to Abbeyfield or staying he would rather be here with us.

"Lots of people have told him how fortunate he was to get a place in the house. It was the first vacancy for over two years and there was competition for it so he realises he was very blessed to get in. Everyone tells him what a lovely room he has and what a lovely set-up it is. But I think that deep down he really isn't convinced.

'All we are left with is a resolution . . . of sorts."

Anthea's story

Anthea's dying brain cells are gradually causing the closing down of her world, and her Ofcaps, Bob and Kate, know they must soon find a place for her in a home where she will be secure and have specialist care.

The idea has been introduced into conversations and Kate has used the attractive euphemism of Hotel for the Older Person in the hope of making 'a room in a home' seem more acceptable. She and Anthea have been invited to dinner at the home that she and Bob have chosen, but, as Kate says, "Although there is a nice invitation on the mantelpiece, I know she smells a rat. I bet there's a scene and I have to pack her into the car to get her there. The woman who runs the place says it would be great to get Mum accustomed to the home before she moves in. We'll see."

People with dementia don't volunteer to go into a home, which makes it very difficult for the carer who must make the decision. Someone with arthritis who can't cope with personal care any more will recognise that they may need some support. But the very nature of dementia is that it stops the person seeing their need and so they deny any problems exist. Few families actually want to take the responsibility for putting Mum or Dad into care as it can seem an act of such finality. Ofcaps also feel a lot of guilt and consider themselves to have failed. These can be harder times than when a parent dies. Death often comes as a relief, even though it's the disease process that you really want to come to an end, not the person.

Until the time comes for the move, Kate is continuing as her mother's carer, a role which is more and more reminiscent of her days as a young mother. The difference then was that her babies, although almost helpless, were rapidly acquiring new skills. Now, the sadness comes with seeing her own Mother losing her skills and becoming virtually helpless.

Anthea's now-limited verbal skills frequently surprise. Sometimes she'll recite poetry or chunks of prose, other times she'll indulge in a lot of lewd language and enjoy uncharacteristic lavatorial humour. On some occasions she'll speak in fluent French, or she might simply repeat, with nerve-jangling frequency, one of her favourite questions: 'Do you have any plans?' Other favourites are the word 'sorted' and the somewhat unlikely 'You can buy a screw from B&Q'.

If Kate is run ragged physically, she does have some time for thinking, even if it is when she's singing to Anthea in the bath, changing urine-soaked clothing or bedding, preparing meals that get pushed about and played with, or listening to that familiar childhood soundtrack for the umpteenth time.

"Sometimes Mum will thank me and say she thinks I do too much," Kate says. "She has no idea why I am doing things – except sometimes when it gets too much for her and she shouts at me saying I'm bossy. Last night, for instance, it wasn't until 10pm that she started saying how horrible I am and how I should be nicer to her. So, once again, I went to bed in despair – but at least most of the day had been good.

"I am often in despair. I get very, very low, and I often feel very alone. When I went into this, when I moved in with Mum, I wondered if the experience of being a carer might make me a better person. I don't think it has. I am still impatient, bad tempered when tired, and self-centred.

"The fact that Mum has been unable to acknowledge or accept the fact that anything at all is wrong with her means she has repelled all kinds of help that would in turn have helped me.

"I have learnt not to bottle anything up but to find an ally and talk, talk, talk. And I laugh a lot, too. There's plenty to be sad about but just as much to have a giggle about and Mum and I like to have a laugh sometimes, even if she isn't too sure what it is that's amusing us."

Put some thought into preparing Mum or Dad for going into the home. Get the rest of the family to help compile a memory book, a kind of personal social history, containing photographs and a potted biography so the staff at the home will know a little of their past and will be able to talk with them about it. A simple photograph album with just one picture from each era is enough. Any more is unnecessarily confusing. Basically, you're aiming as far as you can to try and reinforce their early memories.

The rest of your Mum or Dad's experiences in a care home are likely to be very unsettling from the moment they move in because so much new learning is required, from knowing which is their room to finding it again once they've closed the door. You need to be braced to expect a considerable deterioration in your parent's condition at this time.

Kate says she is very aware of the need to try and have a life of her own, but is happy to be making the sacrifice even though it means that at the moment her life is on hold. "But this is another sort of a life and it's OK," she says. "It's bearable. It has taught me a lot and I've got an intensely close relationship with my Mum that I would never have had otherwise. I continually remind myself that it may be dreadful for me, but it is equally dreadful for Mum.

"The guilt is not good, though, and not easy to live with. I feel guilt that I never encouraged Mum to make the best use of her talents when it would have been possible years ago, and I feel guilt that I was a terrible, argumentative teenager who caused her all sorts of heartache."

Bob's involvement has declined as his Mother's condition has worsened. In the past six months, for example, he has visited only once. "His attitude is very different," says Kate. "I once rang him up and said he had to get more involved again but he finds it difficult. He can't really cope with seeing Mum the way she is. It upsets him too much. He just can't communicate with her any more.

"He knows all the latest legislation on the care of dementia patients, but cannot actually do the caring. I suppose it's a classic defining of the brother/sister roles."

As for Anthea's future, which Kate says she views "with utter bleakness", it is likely to involve issues that at the moment terrify her. "I do hate the fact that so many drugs seem to make them just go on, but I could never play God and decide whether a life should be terminated. That would be unthinkable.

"At the moment, Mum thinks she has a marvellous life. I've asked her if she would like to step off it and she said no, she was enjoying it!"

CHAPTER 6

Who cares for the carers?

"It's the cared for who are looked after, not the carer" – an exasperated Ofcap

Thanks to the legions of unpaid carers in the UK, the National Health Service saves £57 billion every year – the same amount that it would cost to run another entire NHS. That gives an idea of the financial worth of carers, yet their real value is incalculable.

Many of them, by giving up an income, pension rights and prospects of employment, are committing to a future life of poverty or, at best, much reduced circumstances.

So who cares for the carers?

Quite a lot of people care for them – but not many know it. Out there, in the world where lives go on being lived in ordinary ways, just like yours used to, there are all sorts of organisations – state sector, commercial and voluntary – which exist to help people like you.

The trouble is, only a small proportion of Ofcaps are aware of them and even if they were they simply do not have the time to go out and get the help. Instead, support services that could be such a valuable lifeline go unnoticed and unused because the Ofcaps who would benefit are quietly drowning in a sea of fuddled exhaustion, their heads kept up only by the knowledge that they can't, they absolutely can't, slacken their resolve. "I don't even have the time to put my head in my hands and cry," one Ofcap says.

Most people go home after a day's work. Even paid carers walk away when their shift ends, but those who care for family members are never off duty. As if this were not enough, nearly half of all carers juggle their role with paid work and most suffer from any or all of the following: financial worries, emotional stress, depression, physical demands, isolation and loneliness and lack of information and support. Little wonder they need help – but how do they get it?

The simplest and most obvious way to get help is to ask for it. But you need to know what to ask for. Who should be telling you? Just about anybody you or your parent encounters in the NHS, starting with the GP and including all those uniformed or non-uniformed people, with or without name badges, encountered along the way, plus anyone and everyone you encounter in social services. Why aren't you being told? Usually because each person thinks someone else will tell you and anyway they're too busy at the moment so maybe next time will do. It is also quite possible you are being told a little of what you need to know, but the time and the moment are wrong, the circumstances too traumatic, for such information to sink in.

Caring is stressful because the work is draining, the hours are long – often round-the-clock – and the likelihood of a holiday, a long weekend away, or even a quick visit to the dentist, all seem impossible. There are strains, too, on relationships with the rest of the family. In extreme cases this can cause marriage breakdowns and family rifts, so Ofcaps have to tiptoe their way across these minefields with immense sensitivity.

When the role of caring causes lost opportunity and conflicts with paid work, affecting income and pension prospects, the mix of stress and resentment becomes potent. A life on benefits is a poor reward for an Ofcap who has given up a decent job to become a carer.

Recognising that too many carers face poverty, isolation and have little recognition or status, the campaigning charity Carers UK demanded greater recognition of the plight of carers. The result, after a long campaign, was the Carers (Equal Opportunities) Act 2004, which came into force in April 2005. It builds on existing legislation and Government support for carers to ensure they are able to take up opportunities which those without caring responsibilities take for granted.

In short, it is intended to:

- Ensure that all carers know that they are entitled to an assessment of their needs

- Place a duty on councils to consider the carer's outside interests, work, study or leisure when carrying out an assessment

- Promote better joint working between councils and the health service to ensure support for carers is delivered in a coherent manner

When the Act passed through Parliament in 2004, the then Health Minister Stephen Ladyman, said: "Support for carers must revolve around ensuring they are able to make choices as individuals."

Do carers, seriously, have the opportunity to 'make choices as individuals'? According to Deborah, who has given up a full time teaching career to look after her Mother, who has Parkinson's disease, there were choices available to her but she couldn't afford any of them. These included keeping on her job and paying to put her Mother in a residential home or very sheltered living accommodation, or paying for several hours of care each day. "Yes, I had choices," she says, "but they were limited and, to be honest, the decision was made for me on financial grounds. The only way genuine choices are going to be available to carers is if the financial aspect of caring is addressed. Until then, people like me will go on using up their own and their parents' savings while we provide the service that the NHS doesn't." Deborah acknowledges immense support from her local branch of The Parkinson's Disease Association (Helpline: 0800 800 0303 **www.parkinsons.org.uk**).

Steve, a bachelor who moved in with his disabled Father when his parents divorced 12 years ago, says he has given up any hope of the NHS and social care services taking notice of his plight. He cares for his Father round-the-clock, turning him at night, dealing with all his personal hygiene, taking him on bus outings, devising 101 ways of keeping up his spirits and budgeting almost fanatically to ensure they remain just about solvent.

What he says he would like, above all, is someone to recognise what he is doing and to offer him the choice of carrying on or of fulfilling his ambition to become a self-employed computer troubleshooter. He knows that, realistically, he is trapped but he wishes there could be a little less talk and a lot more action on behalf of carers. He has found great support from the Carers UK organisation and is impressed by its campaigning stance. He has frequently sought advice from its carers' helpline (0808 808 7777 Wed and Thurs 10am-noon and 2pm-4pm) and, in his limited spare time, he posts messages on the forum of the Carers UK website (**www.carersuk.org**) and corresponds via email with several other carers. "When I'm really in despair, the only things that keep me going are knowing there are others doing the same sort of drudgery as I'm doing, and that someone might have posted a reply to one of my messages on the forum. It isn't any sort of a life, though."

So many carers have to suffer quietly because they have neither the time nor the opportunity to make a fuss or have their own needs attended to. Mental health problems such as depression are likely to afflict half of all those who provide a high level of care, but very few of them ever get the chance to tell their GPs.

However, lest you feel that virtually every Ofcap in a serious caring role is run ragged and exists in a permanent black cloud of gloom, rest assured that there are many who don't get into this state. True, they tend to be the ones who have sufficient money to throw at the problem – perhaps they buy in enough paid care to give themselves breaks of a decent length, or they have high quality disabled living aids which take away much of the physical strain, but it does very much depend on the circumstances and the *dramatis personae*. And remember, all the money in the world won't take away the worry, which is what wears down many Ofcaps.

Ways to help prevent and manage this worry and stress are vital in an Ofcap's armoury, as is access to direct services for Mum or Dad, in day care, respite care or home support.

Try as it might, the NHS isn't very good at joined up thinking or joined up activity of any sort. This is partly because everyone has greater expectations of what is possible from so-called improvements in technology and we think everything should go smoothly. The NHS and other care organisations are just not able to keep up with these expectations.

Furthermore, those very support organisations can be stretched to breaking point, so great is the burden on their thinly spread resources so it tends to be a lottery, depending on where your parent lives and what their circumstances are.

When your Mum or Dad is sent home from hospital with a chronic ailment that will render them virtually housebound, the expectation is that support services will have been informed. But it happens only occasionally that a fully effective chain of action clunks into place, prompted by a message from the hospital to the GP practice and on to the health visitor, to the occupational therapist, to the many other people and services that could make the patient's life so very much easier.

In theory, this is meant to happen. In practice, as virtually every Ofcap I have ever known would testify, it doesn't. So you have to make it happen. Get busy on the phone, nag, cajole and plead – and then do it again as many times as necessary, until you feel the right level of care is in place for your parent – and for YOU. As a carer you have rights, so there is no need to think you are sub-human, even if exhaustion and The System combine to make you feel as though you are.

Exactly where are the substitutes for you, when you feel you just can't go on any more – or you just need to get out from under? Take heart. They are there, these saints and angels who can fly to your rescue, but they can be a bit backward in coming forward. Your Mum or Dad's GP or social care worker should hopefully be able to point you in the right direction, but as so many of the more helpful organisations are run by part time volunteers you shouldn't expect to strike lucky on your first foray. When you do, it will almost certainly be rewarding.

If there is a carers' centre in your area this could be your first port of call. The Princess Royal Trust for Carers, for example, runs 113 carers' centres, which offer a variety of help from yoga groups to advice sessions. Some also offer pamper days, outings and stress management courses. Feeling better already? Those who work for the Trust are on your side so they will do a lot of your battling for you. So will the people at Age Concern and Carers UK and many other organisations that you probably had no idea even existed.

Provision of voluntary help can be patchy in some areas, but that's where telephones and the internet come into play. Get busy and make contact with some of the organisations mentioned in this book. Whip up help from wherever you can get it. Cash in those vague offers from friends who say, a little dismissively: "Call me if you need me, won't you?" Call them. You need them.

You also need the following if you're going to be an efficient and effective Ofcap without crumbling tendencies:

- Information – on what's available in the way of services, support groups, benefits

- Advice and advocacy – to access and negotiate with local services

- Time off – for holidays, days out or a break from routine

- To meet others – talking to other carers can be a lifeline

- Therapies – stress relief therapies, like massage and aromatherapy, aid relaxation and give you a break

- Stress management – devise ways to deal with your stress before it gets you down

As much as the NHS relies on Ofcaps, so too do all those grateful parents – as this book has illustrated. The NHS can surround itself with as many schemes and dreams as it likes, but the fact remains that for most older people, ill or not, there is no place like home. As one 82 year old former senior school headmistress, who has diabetes, a chronic back complaint and arthritis, says: "I am fortunate that I have enough put by to ensure I'll be able to pay for full time care in my home if I should need it. I've told my son I'm definitely staying put. I live in a granny annexe next to his house, and he understands how strongly I feel about not wanting to go into a home. After all, you can't beat having your own chair and your own room. And your own toilet."

The longer we remain fit, well and, let's face it, breathing, the more certain we can be that decrepitude beckons. There's an inevitability about the fact that if we don't wake up tomorrow with some ailment or another, there's a strong chance it will make its presence felt the day after. What the medical profession is so skilfully doing is postponing the usual sort of mid-life illnesses by, for example, reducing the amount of cardiac disease. This means there are fewer people being hospitalised with heart attacks and strokes. But this only serves to postpone the inevitable and people will get other more chronic degenerative problems which will land them in hospital later in their lives. We're going to live longer, but we'll be more ill in the later stages – which means we'll need more care when we're old.

Present medical practices are simply putting the lid on a time bomb, one hospital consultant says.

So what do we do? How do we safeguard our own futures? Do we bind our children ever closer to us, or do we put our name down now for the bed with the best view in the nearest nursing home?

Let's look on the bright side and take the view of Derek, who says he feels very relaxed about old age. He and his wife, who are both 75, have given enduring power of attorney to their four children "in case we go ga-ga" he says. "You tend to think about things differently when you are 75 from when you're 35. Death can be frightening to people at that age when they think about it. But when you're 75 you know it's going to happen and you are close to other people who you see managing quite well and dying quite happily.

"You just hope that your children will sort things out in a civilised kind of way. We've made simple wills with a trust fund for each of the six grandchildren. We've gone to some lengths to try and avoid conflict situations.

"Quite honestly, the best gift you can give your children is your own independence from them: social, financial and emotional."

Contact us

You're welcome to contact White Ladder Press if you have any questions or comments for either us or the authors. Please use whichever of the following routes suits you.

Phone: 01803 813343 between 9am and 5.30pm

Email: enquiries@whiteladderpress.com

Fax: 01803 813928

Address: White Ladder Press, Great Ambrook,
Near Ipplepen, Devon TQ12 5UL

Website: www.whiteladderpress.com

What can our website do for you?

If you want more information about any of our books, you'll find it at **www.whiteladderpress.com**. In particular you'll find extracts from each of our books, and reviews of those that are already published. We also run special offers on future titles if you order online before publication. And you can request a copy of our free catalogue.

Many of our books have links pages, useful addresses and so on relevant to the subject of the book. You'll also find out a bit more about us and, if you're a writer yourself, you'll find our submission guidelines for authors. So please check us out and let us know if you have any comments, questions or suggestions.

Fancy another good read?

If you've found this book helpful, you might like a sample of one of our other books. *At a **Stroke** The rollercoaster of living with someone who has had a stroke* is the author's account of the aftermath of his wife's stroke.

Huw Watkins' wife suffered a brainstem stroke. For the next six months he found himself on an emotional rollercoaster as he looked after her, and learnt to look after himself at the same time. He had to:

- deal with the medical professionals
- cope with his own deep emotions
- communicate with family and friends
- grasp a whole raft of new knowledge about the illness

Carers of stroke patients are often overlooked as everyone focuses on the patient themselves. This is Huw's own story, together with helpful advice for other carers of stroke patients.

"This is a wonderful book. There is humanity & good sense in this true story, rare qualities desperately needed to combat the despair of sudden, powerful illness. How I wish I could have read it when I was caring for my mother." **Miriam Margolyes**

At a Stroke is priced at £7.99 and, as well as being on sale in bookshops, is available (with free p&p) from White Ladder Press on 01803 813343 or **www.whiteladderpress.com**.

At a Stroke

EXTRACT

Fourth Week of May

The GP's car drew up outside. I felt a great sense of relief; someone seeing Dilys at last. The GP sat on the side of the bed, as pleasant and as cheerful as ever, putting Dilys at ease at once, chatting away about the weather and telling Dilys about her children. Blood pressure, temperature – both fine, she found. It was the teeth and mouth problem that exercised her most, and after a careful examination, she diagnosed a case of thrush, and prescribed antibiotics and a mouthwash. For the constipation, which was worrying Dilys, she arranged for the nurse to call and administer an enema.

"Come and see me on Tuesday," the GP said to Dilys. I felt a weight lifting off my shoulders. The doctor was clearly expecting a rapid improvement.

I hurried to the chemist, and we started the treatment at once.

The nurse came the following day, a lively, talkative lady, who soon dispelled any embarrassment Dilys felt over the enema. It was the day that would have been the start of our family holiday in Majorca, a holiday I'd had to cancel a few weeks ago, when Dilys had started to feel unwell. The nurse was encouraging.

"You were wise to cancel," she said. "It's a lovely island, and you'll enjoy it so much more when you're both fit."

The company seemed to be doing Dilys good. For the moment, her old self peeped out from behind the curtain of her illness, a glimpse of the lively, sociable, clear voiced person I knew so well.

To cheer Dilys up I began to talk about where she'd like to go when she was better.

"Somewhere in this country at first," she thought. "The Lakes – I've always liked the Lakes." I talked about some of our various holidays there, renting cottages in Coniston and Dunnerdale, staying in Langdale, and our last trip there, a jolly weekend with a lot of friends near Ambleside.

"Definitely the Lakes," she said. Then the nurse left, and she fell back to sleep.

The weekend passed without any obvious change in the feeling in Dilys's throat.

"It takes a couple of days for the antibiotic to work," I encouraged her.

The boys and their families had now arrived in Majorca, where we would all have been on holiday together, and they rang us.

"Much the same," I answered. "Still resting in bed, but the doctor's been and she's on tablets now."

"And how about you?" they asked.

"Oh I'm fine." They sounded reassured.

Calls from the children really help. Knowing that someone else is concerned about the invalid eases the pressure of your concern: others share it with you. And it's a good feeling to know that they're thinking of you, too.

On Monday, for the first time, she wanted an arm to walk the five steps to the toilet. "I'm feeling very wobbly," she said, "and I don't want to fall." Our bedroom has an en suite bathroom, and the toilet is five paces from the bed. Yet when she went to urinate, she now needed my arm for those five paces. Why is her walking deteriorating, I wondered. Is it just weakness, or something more?

I felt a sudden hollow, helpless feeling. The relief at the doctor's optimism dwindled and the worry I had felt last week reappeared, joined by a sense of foreboding. Still hardly eating, and now the walking beginning to go? Later in the day, after half a bowl of soup for lunch, she thought she'd get up again, and sit in her favourite window seat. She took my arm again, and we started for the lounge. I noticed how slowly she was walking, and when we got to the hall, a few yards away, she asked to sit down. "I need a little rest," she said. After a minute or two she started again, and we reached the lounge.

It was a beautiful day; across the valley the sun shone on the hills to the south, and the flowers she loved in the garden were sitting up as if in salute. "It's no good," she said after 10 minutes, "I've got to get back to bed." She slept for the rest of the day. It was if she'd had an energetic workout: but she'd just walked 20 yards, with great difficulty. I cancelled a day trip we had booked for the following week.

If you're worried about calling the doctor yet again, don't forget the NHS Direct helpline. There's always a trained person there to talk things through with you. The phone number is in the Helpline page at the front of the telephone directory.

"Washing day," Dilys reminded me.

"Put in the powder and press the button?" I asked uncertainly. At least I knew where the machine was, and it ought to be foolproof.

She nodded. "No need to change the programme."

Thank the Lord for that, I thought. I had done the washing occasionally in the past, and now wasn't the time to have to learn the intricacies of the household gadgets. I was a member of that older generation where household tasks were strictly the responsibility of the females, and apart from a long ago year at university, I'd not looked after myself. I felt that camping trips in the wild had made me pretty self-sufficient, but washing clothes in a stream and cooking over a primus stove wasn't the best of training for running a household with an invalid.

There was no change the next morning, except that the pain in her eye was worse. I rang the medical centre and waited till the end of the morning, when the doctor rang back.

"I'll arrange an appointment this afternoon for the eye clinic," she said. She explained about the need to check for arteritis, a possible complication of the polymyalgia from which Dilys had been steadily recovering.

"But I can't get her there without an ambulance."

I described her difficulties in getting to the lounge. Trying to dress her, getting her to the car, walking from the hospital car park into the main building...impossible. The doctor thought for a moment.

"We'll check via a blood test," she said. "I'll get the nurse to call in this afternoon to take a sample, and if you can get the sample to the path lab I'll ask for an urgent test. They'll phone me with the results and I'll let you know tomorrow."

The nurse came that afternoon. Before I drove off to catch the hospital pathology lab with the blood sample, nurse asked if I would like her to arrange a wheelchair for Dilys.

Dilys in a wheelchair? After all these years of health, had poor

Dilys suddenly come to this? It was another blow: but of course it made sense. I agreed to fetch the chair from a centre some 20 miles away the next morning, and drove off for the path lab.

Next day everything seemed to happen. I left Dilys, who still wasn't eating breakfast, found the wheelchair centre without too much difficulty and returned to her. When I returned, we tried to chat for a while, and, oh dear, I noticed a slight slurring in her speech. Yet another blow. What was going on, I wondered. Later, she asked for help to get to the toilet, but she wasn't able to get there in time. The dreaded word 'incontinence' flashed through my mind. Was this just a one-off, or the shape of things to come? Foreboding grew. Then the doctor rang.

"The tests are completely clear," she said. Perhaps I should have been glad that the possible arteritis had been excluded; in fact I was much more worried that the cause of Dilys's illness had not been identified. I couldn't wait to describe the latest symptoms to the doctor. There was a distinct pause.

Most people think of a serious stroke as a sudden, devastating loss of functions. This is often the case, but not always. When someone has already suffered from TIAs, or is known to be vulnerable to a stroke, that possibility must always be considered. Those of us who are not medicals are unlikely to be aware of the range of symptoms which might indicate a stroke and to be able to distinguish them from other possibilities.

"I'll call to see her tomorrow," she said.

True to her word, the GP arrived in the morning. When I opened the door to her, she stopped in the hall before going into the bedroom.

"I'm beginning to be concerned about Dilys," she warned. My sense of foreboding became overwhelming, and I rapidly rattled off my worries.

"So many of her functions – walking, speech, bladder control, all these now seem to be deteriorating," I stated anxiously, "as well as the original problems, the loss of appetite and pain round the side of her head and eye."

"Sometimes minor problems can mask something more serious," she continued, "and I might have to suggest admission to hospital. How would you feel about that?"

I felt a sense of relief that something more was being done, and said so.

"Then let's talk to Dilys together," she said.

Index